MEMORIES

By Rita Williams

www.bryngoldbooks.com

First published in Great Britain in 2010
by Bryngold Books Ltd.,
100 Brynau Wood, Cimla,
Neath, South Wales SA11 3YQ.

www.bryngoldbooks.com

Typesetting, layout,
editing and design
by Bryngold Books

ISBN 978-1-905900-20-6

Contents

About the author	4
Foreword	5
Introduction	6
Around and about	7
Colourful characters	31
School report	49
Shining stars	67
Times of toil	73
May Day magic	91
Happy times	101
Worshipful days	127
Sporting spirit	141
Ace of clubs	159

About the author

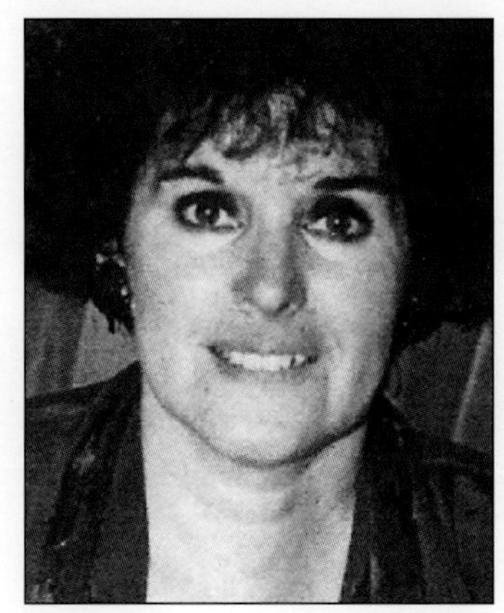

Rita Williams was born and brought up in Tyn-y-Graig mansion high on the mountainside above Crynant in the Dulais Valley. She is proud that happy memories of her childhood days growing up there with her younger brother Vincent have remained with her throughout her life. She describes it as a wonderful place in which to grow up.

Rita's mother was a Londoner who as young woman became a member of the Salvation Army and trained at the William Booth Memorial College. In 1935, at a passing out parade in the Albert Hall, she was given marching orders that brought her to Seven Sisters. It was here that she met, fell in love and married Rita's father, who was a miner. The couple made their home at Tyn-y-Graig.

A former pupil of Neath Girls' Grammar School Rita's first job was with prominent Neath Photographer HG Lewis. This was followed by employment in the offices of the Evans Bevan Vale of Neath Brewery at Cadoxton. She later worked for the Neath Guardian and South Wales Evening Post newspapers. Her brother Vince was also involved in the newspaper industry for 40 years. Little did she realise at the time, that when she joined the Neath Guardian she was taking the first steps on the path that would lead to the creation of this book.

Rita noticed that many districts had their own local news columns, but not the Melin and decided to do something about it. She asked the editor, Elfed Rees, himself a man with strong Melin links, if she could provide one and he agreed. So in 1980 she began what was to become almost 30 years of reporting Melin matters. During this time Rita immersed herself in the community and its activities, listened to countless residents with fascinating stories to tell, some happy, some sad and shared them with her readers far and wide. Their warmth and hospitality was second to none. For many with an interest in the Melin it was a communication link all of its own. To turn some of the information she gleaned into a book is a long-held ambition she feels proud to have finally achieved.

Dedication

I would like to dedicate this book to the five wonderful men in my life, my husband Terry, sons Kevin and Richard and grandsons Ben and Joseph.

Foreword

I was delighted to be invited to provide the foreword for a book on the Melin by my old friend Rita Williams. At one time we were in regular contact, when I was a local Councillor and Rita was writing her interesting newspaper columns on which this book is based.

During my time as Leader of Neath Port Talbot Council, I saw all the distinctive communities that go to make up our wonderful county borough. The Melin is one of the most distinctive of these and full of special people and places.

Living in the community and being involved with so many things Rita was ideally placed to write the Grapevine column for the area. She definitely had her finger on the Melin pulse. It is because of this that her column, over 30 years, recorded and advertised all the special events and activities that went on.

The people who took part in them were also important as they were the ones who organised things and made the community what it was and indeed still is today.

Her column not only publicised events, but also passed on congratulations at times of joy such as anniversaries, weddings, births and birthdays. Of course, there were also deaths to announce too. Looking back now, Rita's column was an important source of news for the people living in the Melin. It was therefore a great shame that it was brought to an end in 2009.

Despite this the Melin community spirit lives on with the many organisations in the area playing their part. Before finishing as council leader I was able to announce that the Melin was to become a Housing Renewal Area which will improve things further.

Most importantly the people of the Melin will ensure its future.

As for Rita, she has ensured through this book we remember the past too. Well done Rita.

DEREK VAUGHAN

Member of the European Parliament

Acknowledgements

It has been a pleasure and a delight to write for the people of the Melin, and I thank everyone for the news they provided, the fascinating anecdotes and the wonderful old photographs they shared. This book is made up of a selection of those stories and photographs and once again I would like to thank all those who have helped make it possible. This includes everyone who helped with the background information on the photographs and tracking down the names of some of those on them. This was not an easy task, particularly when some go back almost a century. I have tried hard to ensure that all the details are correct, but will apologise in advance for any inaccuracies with names or dates, and the poor condition of some of the photographs.

Special thanks to Bill Adams,

Michaela Locke and Fay Harris together with the staff of Bryngold Books. I really could not have accomplished this without the help of you all.

Introduction

Melincrthyan — or the Melin as it is affectionately referred to — is a Neath community that can lay claim to a long and interesting past.

Some of this is hinted at on the pages of Melin Memories which is not so much a history of this special place, but more a miscellany reflecting the people, places and events that have played a part, however small, in its development. The stories and photographs have been drawn from the columns I wrote for the Neath Guardian, Evening Post and Courier newspapers down three decades. Often they drew comment from readers far and wide.

Combined together these historical facts, fascinating memories, salutes to achievement, tales of heroism, stories of industry, trade and the community at large, portray just how important a part the Melin has played in the world. There are recollections of some of the area's colourful characters along with others who have embarked on a quest that brought them fame and fortune whatever career path in life they chose to follow.

Alongside this, school days, work, sport and entertainment creep in to the recollections of life in the Melin that feature on the following pages. The popular and enjoyable May Day events earn their place too.

Add all these things together and the result is a compendium of life in our busy community, something that I hope everyone will enjoy dipping in to..

Rita Williams, 2010

Chapter 1

Around and about

When it comes to questions, there is one that is probably asked more frequently than most by many of the people who live in one of Neath's longest established districts.

Though it played an important part in the industrial history of the town and its origins can be traced far back in time there are few, to this day, who would pin their money on whether it should be Melin with an 'i' or Melin with a 'y'.

It will need no explaining to Welsh speakers that melin with an 'i' translates as mill in English, while melin with a 'y' means yellow.

The question has cropped up regularly during the 50 years or so that I have lived in the area. During the 30 of those that I was a newspaper correspondent I lost track of the number of readers of my column who rang me up to inform me that I had mis-spelt Melyncryddan.

Now though, with the column itself consigned to history, perhaps I have the answer for them — it seems it can be spelt either way!

At least that is the information I gleaned, along with other attentive listeners, at a fascinating slide show and talk presented by historian Clive Reed in which he shared some fascinating information.

It seems that the earliest known reference to a mill in the area was in 1295, when the 'Mill of Credan' was recorded. This was a grist or corn mill for grinding corn to produce flour. Credan was very probably a person's name, hence mill of Credan. He could possibly have been an immigrant who came to the new Norman town of Neath and set up his trade as a miller on the stream which now bears his name Credan or Cryddan.

The corn mill was still operating on the stream in 1658 and was referred to as Crethan's Mill. New corn mills were erected by the Mackworth family in 1776 and their lease refers to the Melincrythan Mill. The last corn mill on the Cryddan stream was the Bush Mill, which was in operation during the Victorian era. All these mills were known as Melin in the Welsh language. A tucking mill for the manufacture of flannel is also recorded on the stream in 1666.

In 1695, a new industry appeared on the Cryddan brook. The Mackworth's copperworks. This used the Cryddan water to operate a large waterwheel in the factory for crushing copper ores and to operate a bellows to produce a blast of air for the furnaces. The construction of this works required the destruction of the tucking mill.

The waste from the copper smelting process would have been dumped close to the works and this would eventually contaminate the stream and colour it green or yellow. Copper workers were recorded as living at Melincrythan Cottages in 1776.

A chemical works was recorded on the east bank of the stream in 1798. This produced vitriol or sulphuric acid. The sulphur would have been imported by sailing ships to a wharf on the River Neath near its junction with the Melincrythan Pill. The waste polluted the river and the

A panorama of the heart of Melincrythan.

Melincrythan stream, again turning the water yellow, melyn in the Welsh language. Maps of Neath dated 1844 identify the Melin area as Melyn Cryddan, the yellow Cryddan. The census of 1841 also records Melyncrythan. To people living in the locality during that period, the stream would have been referred to as the Melyn Cryddan, or the yellow Cryddan. Other heavy industries were also established in the area due to the abundance of coal which was mined locally. The Penrhiwtyn Ironworks 1792, Eaglesbush Foundry, 1838, Milllands Brick and Tile Works around 1860, Melin Forge 1864, Melin Tinplate Works 1864, Eaglesbush Tinplate Works 1890, Neath Steel Sheet and Galvanizing Works 1896, Cambrian Brick and Pottery Works around 1890.

The Metal Box Company came in 1937, and post Second World War developments, included David S Smith Packaging Ltd in1947, the Metal Spinning Company circa 1950, and in more recent times the Millands Industrial Estate.

All the earlier industries needed housing for their workers in the form of terraced cottages. Some of the earliest houses were in Bowen Street, Bush Row and

This was Springfield Terrace near Stockham's Corner before the Methodist Church was built. Work on the church started in 1913 and it opened in 1914. Notice the houses decorated with bunting. This was either for Queen Victoria's Diamond Jubilee in 1897; when her son became King Edward VII in 1901 or for his Coronation on August 9, 1902. One person who was interested in this old photo was Chris Stephens from Harle Street who previously lived at Bangor House in Lewis Road, near the terrace. In 1900, her great- grandparents Thomas and Jane Davies came from Bangor to Neath where he ran a licensed flannel dealers in Gold Street. The business later moved to Windsor Road before he started the Osborne Bus Company and the family finally moved to Lewis Road. In the picture of the church, opposite, the houses at either end of the terrace can just be seen each side of the church building.

Mile End Row. As time went on, the various landowners, important personages, and industrial entrepreneurs gave their names to the new streets and roads. Herbert Road, Evans Road, Walters Road, Gardeners Lane, Cecil Street, Ethel Street, Henry Street and Pendrill Street.

Marshfield Road took its name from the Eaglesbush Marsh, while Southgate Street was the location of the south gate of the Turnpike Trust. The residents of those streets required service industries in the form of small shops, which were created by adapting the front rooms of their homes. Churches, chapels, schools and social institutions were added later which all combined to create the community known as the Melin/Melyn. On reaching the 21st Century, we see a vast change to the face of the Melin. The disappearance of much of the heavy industry, the demise of all the wonderful small shops and businesses, and the dwindling of many public houses, mostly replaced by flats. Our churches and chapels have withstood the passing of time. We still have Ebenezer, Herbert Road, St Catherine's Church, Siloh, Elim Pentecostal, New Maria Congregational and the Methodist Church at Stockham's Corner.

Neath Methodist Church, with the houses at either end of Springfield Terrace just visible.

This was the Melin Post Office in 1912. It was situated on the corner of Marshfield Road and Briton Ferry Road and the home at one time of Annie and John James. Annie was the daughter of David Thomas a Neath station master. The delightful picture opposite shows the ironmongers of Idris Jones in 1908. It too later saw service as the Melin Post Office. The building doesn't seem to have changed much down the years. May Lewis from Southgate Street loaned the photograph. Her grandfather, Charlie Davies, of Florence Street is on the left, with Idris Jones himself. Charlie's young son Richard (Dick) Davies is in front. What a wonderful display of hardware there was for customers to see. The picture below shows the Hong Kong Stores in Briton Ferry Road around 1886. It was situated between Marshfield Road and Bowen Street, opposite what is now Neath Boys and Girls Club.

The ironmongery store of Idris Jones, Briton Ferry Road, 1908.

Standing in the doorway of his shop in 1890 is Davies the Fruitier. The shop was on the corner of Southgate Street and Briton Ferry Road. Robert Davies from Cotton Court, who was a lorry boy with Western Fruit, in 1953, recalls the shop being called Davies the Gardener and believes that the man in the photograph had a son who was gassed in the First World War.

The street where you could buy almost anything!

Len Palfrey recalled the shops on the stretch of road between Southgate Street and Whittington Street. There was Davies the Gardener on the corner; then Jones the Melin, a draper; next the Dairy, followed by Jim Davies a gent's tailor, then the private house of Mr. Bryan who was a Great Western Railway horsedrawn delivery wagon driver and on the end Joe Spagna's ice cream parlour. Later Jones the Draper took over the dairy and the shop became Jones Leicester House.

Barbara Griffiths of London Road recalled how her mother and grandparents, Henry and Eliza Sophia Lintern, lived in a back room above Davies the Fruiterer's shop. Barbara also told a story her mother told her about the time her grandfather was so ill he was taken by hand ambulance to Neath Station and put on a train for Swansea and the hospital there. Sadly he died of

Rosalina's fashion store, Briton Ferry Road, in the 1960s. It was a popular shop with many Melin women.

appendicitis. A bad memory she had was how in those days the coffin was placed in the home and with only the one room at the back of the shop Henry was laid out in their living room for some days.

Another interesting story that is recalled by Barbara is about her Mother, Annie, when she worked in the Victoria laundry.

A man turned up there one day. He was a Union representative and wanted to have a meeting with the workers to talk about their poor wages. As a result, the first union meeting of the Victoria Laundry was held above this shop and through that meeting the workers had a considerable rise in their wages. Barbara's Mother married Huw Fisher Williams and lived in Southgate Street. He was a conductor on Neath's gas trams.

The photograph above, loaned by Janice Sambrook and taken in the 1960s will revive memories of well loved drapery and women's fashion shop Rosalina's in Briton Ferry Road. It was owned by Janice's mother. It was next to Davies the Fruiterer, son of WH Davies. Janice's mother was in business there of about 25 years.

Rosalina had started up in general drapery in a front room in Lewis Road and built up a successful business. She then moved to Jefferies Stores on the corner of Llewellyn Street, before moving to the more prominent position offered by Leicester House. Janice recalls those happy days in the Melin with faithful customers.

In those distant days it seems you didn't have to go into town to shop as everything could be bought within that small area.

At that time in the 1960s on the opposite corner from John Davies the Fruiterer was Billy Lewis the Butcher, which later became the Pet Shop, then the sweet shop which was run by John and Pam Dawes.

Next door was Reason's the Cobbler, then Pearn's the Furniture Shop. Further along was Charles the Chemist. Billy Bowen the Butcher was next. What a character he was. His meat, he claimed, came from his aunt's farm in Brecon and was the best. Next to him was the cafe, then came Fisher's the Chemist where his assistants would give you good advice on your prescriptions and medicines. You could also weigh your baby on their infant scales.

Also along there was Beasley's the Barbers, an ironmongery, and who could possibly forget the warm crusty bread of Stockham's the Master Bakers who made the best cream slices in the area.

They were really halcyon days when we all lived life to the full with respect and personal service — and without a computer in sight.

This postcard view was taken from the hill below Bryn Road, looking down over the Melin before the building of Danygraig Road. The man and boy are standing where it was later constructed. The card was loaned by Darrell Gardiner from Bryn Road. It was sent in 1911 by his grandmother Mrs. Treharne, who lived in Mile End Row, to Darrell's parents, her daughter and son-in-law, Margaret and Ben Gardiner. At the time they were living in a small village near Carmarthen where Ben was a railway signalman. They later moved to Neath. The photograph below was taken almost 100 years later from the same spot. One landmark visible in both pictures is the spire of St Catherine's Church. The houses in Danygraig Road are hiding St Catherine's Parish Hall which is now Melyncrythan Community Centre. The Metal Box Factory and Castle Bingo, are among buildings which have changed the view.

This was how beer was delivered to many local pubs in the 1920s — by burly draymen and a steam-powered lorry! The side of this building in Briton Ferry Road makes no secret of the fact that it housed the London Inn, a once popular hostelry. Showing countless beer barrels, the photograph was loaned by Mrs. Freda Holding, a former landlady of the Royal Exchange pub, a short distance away.

Quenching the thirst of the hard workers

A reader from Tonna informed me that the landlord of the London Inn, before the 1940s was George Barrett. He also told me that Freda's grandfather Harry Arnold, sang behind the silent films that were screened at the Gnoll Cinema and also at the National Eisteddfod, when it was held in Neath in 1934. On that occasion the Eisteddfod pavilion was in Dyfed Road on the site of today's Sports Centre.

Back to the London Inn, and thanks to a call from Janet Tamplin, I discovered that the landlord in the early 1940s was Glyn Jones. He was the eldest brother of her mother, Mrs. Margaret Tamplin of Pentwyn. He was one of seven children, born in Water Street and married May Houlance from Ethel Street. The couple had a son Tommy. Even more information came my way from Ken Chapple of Cadoxton. He recalled that in the mid to late 1940s, Tommy was a boxer and a very popular fighter in professional tournaments that were held in the Gwyn Hall, and also on one occasion on the Gnoll rugby ground. Ken's late father Dick Chapple was the ticket sales secretary of the Neath Boxing Committee, which developed in 1945, from the welcome home committee set up to raise funds for troops returning from the Second World War. Ken was a programme seller at these tournaments and can remember Tommy Jones, as well as other local boxers such as Mel Wathan, Denis (boxer) Williams and Bryn Davies from Skewen.

Another popular Melin hostelry was the Farmers Arms situated on Briton Ferry Road at its junction with Bowen Street. It was another of the places where, after a hard days graft workmen from the local metal industries could relax and enjoy themselves. As you entered the front door there were just wooden floorboards and in the right hand corner which was known as Tattersall's were the punters. The floor in the centre of the room was covered with flagstones and where 'Sooty' a pot bellied stove stood, while at the far end there was a terrazzo floor, where a fruit and veg business operated.

Melin poet Terry Hetherington wrote a number of stories about the Farmers. One in particular relates to an annual event linked to Sooty, the pot bellied stove. "During the

The Farmers Arms, a popular Melin hostelry and home of Sooty the pot-bellied stove.

summer it sat dormant and darkly brooding," he said. "Then, each October it was lit and kept burning day and night throughout winter. The first lighting of Sooty was a great night in the life of the Melin. Local shops displayed hand painted posters proclaiming: All welcome to our annual event, the lighting of Sooty.

"On the night, the Farmers was bursting at the seams. Orders for the best beer were passed overhead to the bar, full glasses returned the same way. Calls of nature during the evening were overcome by shouldering a way to the nearest window, climbing out, walking around the building to the decrepit outside bog at the rear, retracing ones steps and climbing back in, helped by many willing hands.

"The Melin character, I emphasise *the*, because there were many, clad in running shorts and vest, sporting Number 14, was by now running through adjoining streets. He carried a blazing torch and was cheered on by wives and girlfriends, barred from the proceedings. At last, the door would burst open.

"Breathless, torch held high he would stand there bathing in acclaim. A path would painfully be cleared, and with great ceremony, he would advance on Sooty. Not a sound would be heard, the silence in the bar, with so many people packed in, was unbelievable. Flame would be put to kindling, and not until a throaty roar could be heard from sooty's flue pipe would the silence be broken. Then a great burst of song: "Cr-o-o-o-own him, crown him Lord of all." Why this hymn, nobody knew, or tries to reason. It was Sooty's hymn and that was that. In truth, young men had lumps in their throats, old men tears in their eyes, marvelous incongruity."

On the opposite page is a view down Crythan Road with the clock tower of St David's Church visible in the distance. A pub quiz question often asked is: "Which is the only pub in Neath where you can stand by the bar and see the town clock?" The answer is the Builders Arms, from where this picture was taken.

For many years Dorothy Griffiths was the landlady of the Builders Arms, a role that had been taken by her parents before her. Dorothy was a true Melin character, once met, never forgotten.

After the Builders was mentioned in my column, I was contacted by Iris Davies of London Road. She was interested in an article about JP Morgan who had been mentioned in a TV series titled Welsh in New York. He originated from Neath, emigrated to America in the mid 19th Century and became one of the richest men there through banking. Mrs Davies was formally Iris Morgan and brought up in the Builders Arms along with her sisters Dorothy and Peggy.

Iris remembers that her aunt Mary Ann Morgan, who was a spinster, would often visit the Builders and regale drinkers with stories. Mary Ann, from The Green, would tell how vessels came up the River Neath and their captains would stay in the nearby pubs.

Mary Ann also used to tell how her uncle had left Neath, and gone to America, and that one day the family would be rich. Is it a coincidence? I wonder if he was J.P.

The view down Crythan Road from the Builders Arms with the clock tower of St David's Church clearly visible.

Terry John, landlord of the Prince of Wales public house, Briton Ferry Road, Melincrythan, outside the premises in 1967.

Stockhams's Corner, named after Stockham's bakery can be seen on the right of this photograph which was taken at the end of the 19th Century. The business was started in 1888 by William John Stockham who married Sarah Ann Fry of the famous Fry chocolate family. The bakery was later taken over by his son Fred Stockham and after his days was run by their three children, John, Fred and Marian. Stockhams Bakery celebrated its 100th Anniversary on January 31, 1988. It closed in 1989. The picture below shows a fascinating collection of fresh loaves in the window. You can almost smell them! On the right is a series of pictures showing just how much the area around Stockham's Corner has changed in recent times.

It was goodbye to Stockham's bakery at the end of the 20th Century.

With the demolition of Stockham's Bakery and other business premises. This was a rare view for residents of Eva Street who for a while could see the Royal British Legion and the Highlander pub.

Another rare view, this time from Stockham's Corner, looking up Eva Street towards Brookdale Street in the distance.

Stockhams Corner in the 21st Century. Flats have now been built and it is no longer possible to look into Eva Street from this point.

St Joseph's Roman Catholic School in Pendrill Street, 1970. It was demolished in 1972 and a new school opened in Cook Rees Avenue. Many people will have lots of happy memories from those distant school days. Apparently, until the school had a new dinner hall the pupils used to be marched up Bowen Street, across Briton Ferry Road and into Neath Boys Club for their lunch. Some will have not so happy memories of the time during the Second World War when bombs fell on Pendrill Street near the school. The result of this bombing by the German airforce can be seen below. The incident happened on August 20, 1940.

When the Melin led the way on road safety across the borough

The Melin may have many claims to fame, but this is a really unusual one that perhaps not too many of the districts residents will be aware of.

The district can lay claim to the first ever pedestrian zebra crossing in the old Borough of Neath!

The photograph above showing a group of schoolgirls being safely shepherded across Briton Ferry Road was taken around the time, way back in 1950/51, when the zebra crossing was put in place.

It spanned the busy road from the Exchange Public House to Mrs. Butlers Fish and Chip Shop.

Those young girls crossing are Sandra Payne, who loaned the photograph; Pat Brennan, Lynne Richards, Lorna Thompson, Alvine James and Barbara Speare.

The lollipop lady is Molly Richards who was from Evans Road. The Baglan foundry wall can be seen on the right hand side stretching into the distance. On the left is the corner shop that was called Sheila's. Further down was Dr Coyne's surgery and you can also see the Eaglesbush Pub and the start of Mile End Row.

It was these houses that were flooded whenever the Crythan brook overflowed.

Mr. Leslie Finn from Primrose Road remembered the crossing well. He was born next to Butler's fish and chip shop. It had previously been his mother's and grandmother's grocery shop and had then been called Knights. Leslie's father died in 1941 when he was just 10 years old. His mother kept the business going for a number of years, but eventually the family moved a short way down the road to Bush Row. The shop which was on the corner of Chemical Road was later demolished.

This is the swing bridge over the River Neath. It was constructed and brought into use in 1894 and originally carried the double track of the Rhondda and Swansea Bay Railway over the River Neath, about a mile below Cwrt Sart Station and two miles by river from Neath town. Trains still use the bridge, but when the large vessels no longer came up the river, there was little use for the swing bridge. The last known operator of the bridge was Harold Sharp of Westbourne Road. The swing bridge did its last swing sometime after the Second World War. Former signalman Dennis Tucker, based at the Cardonnel junction, remembered the last movement of the bridge, which was for repairs, in 1950 and his colleague at the Dynevor Junction signal box, Graham Lewis, remembered being called upon to open and close the bridge until 1956, just to make sure it was in working condition. it was finally locked out of use in 1972.

The Square Pond, near the Metal Box Factory is something that often puzzles people. How did it come into being? It seems the clay was excavated from the land for use in the construction of the Neath Canal in the late 18th Century. For many years it was a popular fishing pond for local anglers. The swing bridge can just be seen in the background.

This is a peep into the tranquil Eaglesbush Valley, a designated nature reserve. Owned by Neath Port Talbot Council it is a steep sided woodland valley with a brook running through it. The underlying geology is permanent sandstone from the Upper Carboniferous coal measures, producing an acidic soil. The valley provides an interesting combination of historical features, accessible open space and natural habitats supporting rich flora. The Crythan Brook hasn't always been as tranquil as the idyllic view seen above however. On one occasion on Monday, July 18, 1955 the brook burst its banks resulting in devastating floods in the Melin. The picture below shows the former Gourlay's Yard at the entrance to Eaglesbush Valley with water rushing down. The borough suffered from a rainstorm of unprecedented severity. The Mayor of Neath at the time, Alderman Gilbert Rosser opened an appeal fund stating this was the worst catastrophe which had befallen the Borough in living memory.

The capped pit shaft of Eaglesbush Colliery, guarded by railings.

The distant day when disaster struck the Melin

As with many other locationss in South Wales, coal was worked in the Melin. Coal was produced in Cwm Cryddan near Eaglesbush House in 1802 and probably earlier. One of the places that this happened was Eaglesbush Colliery which lay on the other side of the Cryddan Valley to the Westernmoor Colliery. An early manuscript suggests that Mr. Evans, of Eaglesbush, was in partnership there with George Penrose, of Westernmoor Colliery, as early as 1802. The families were later connected by marriage, for in 1833, George Penrose had married Miss Evans, of Eaglesbush, and was in residence there.

In the early days, Eaglesbush coal went by tram road and inclines to be shipped on the canal. Later, it was conveyed over a new tram road to Briton Ferry and shipped from the river bank. The Gnoll and Eaglesbush collieries are mentioned in the 1842 Children's Employment Report and the owners described as Penrose and Evans. At that time, apparently the miners entered the Gnoll Colliery by being lowered into the shaft in a bucket, whereas at the Eaglesbush Colliery they had the option of using a ladder. Apparently, when they descended the shaft by bucket, they did so four or five at a time and there was a fatal accident at Eaglesbush in 1837 when a boy fell out of the bucket, after which they were allowed to enter the mine by a ladder. At the colliery, the coal was brought out from the

Registration District / Dosbarth Cofrestru: Neath

1923. Death in the Sub-district of / Marwolaeth yn Is-ddosbarth: Neath in the / yn Counties of Glamorgan and Brecknock

1		2	3	4	5	6	7	8	9
No.	When and where died	Name and surname	Sex	Age	Occupation	Cause of death	Signature, description and residence of informant	When registered	Signature of registrar
477	Twenty first September 1923 [illegible] Colliery Eaglesbush Valley Neath U.D	Robert Ernest JONES	Male	38 years	of 10A Albany Terrace Llantwit Road Neath U.D Coal Hewer	Fractured Skull accidentally caused by fall of stone at Colliery	Certificate received from B Edward Howe Coroner for Western Division of Glamorgan Inquest held Twenty fourth September 1923	Twenty fifth September 1923	W B Rees Registrar

The Death Certificate of Robert Ernest Jones.

The ruins of the former Eaglesbush Colliery engine house.

SOUTH WALES

Daily Post

ST GENUINE CIRCULATION. SMALL ADS. PRODUCE BEST RESULTS.

SATURDAY, SEPTEMBER 22, 1923 One Penny.

mittee Chairman and Drink

ST V. WEST.

lational Eisteddfod At Hendy.

HE AWARDS.

annual semi-national was held at Hendy on Saturday marquee on a field adjoining Hall, and a great crowd. Many National winners

was the male voice com- "Fallen Heroes" (Cyril as many as eight parties. It was practically a com- East v. West. On Sunday grand concert is to be held at by the famous Romilly and Band, under the con- of Mr. W. M. Williams. The were the officials of the —President. Mr. Evan Wil- "Glyndwr" (High Sheriff of shire and President of the Association); conductor, Harries Williams (rector of); adjudicators: Music, Dr. and Mr. W. D. Clee, (Ystalyfera); literature. Rev. Williams (Monordeify); Mr. Dan Mathews (Pontar- Mrs. Evan Williams ; fancy work, Mrs. Henry (Llwyngwern); accompanists, Thomas and Silas Evans

THE AWARDS.

TO-DAY'S WIRES.

News by Telegraph and Telephone.

SMALL-POX IN LONDON.

Another death from small-pox occurred in London on Friday, the victim being a man living in Battersea.

GERMAN MARKS.

German marks show some recovery in value, the latest quotation being about 737,000,000, or 130,000,000 less to the £ than Friday's closing rate.

CHINESE INDEMNITY.

Peking, Friday.—The Government on Thursday paid over an indemnity of 25,000 gold dollars demanded for the murder of Mr. Colman, an American.

Sick Princesses.

Rome, Saturday.—A slight improvement is reported since yesterday in the condition of Princesses Matalda and Giovanna, who are suffering from typhoid fever at Racconigi.—(Reuter.)

Cloub-burst at Bombay.

During Thursday's tempest twelve inches of rain fell in twenty-four hours at Bombay. Several buildings partially collapsed. In one instance a boy was killed and three women seriously injured.

Prince in Alberta.

The Prince of Wales and his party are spending the week-end at Banff, Alberta. Before His Royal Highness left his ranch on Friday there was a great snow-storm, which held up all work for the time being.

Norwich House Collapse.

There has been a second death as the result of the house collapse at Norwich, Fred Lang, one of the injured, dying in hospital on Saturday morning.

STONE ON HEAD.

Local Collier's Terrible Death.

NEATH FATALITY.

Robert Ernest Jones (36), of 107, Albany-terrace, Llantwit-road, Neath, was killed on Friday afternoon. He was working, together with two colleagues on the Treany Seam, a small seam in the EaglesBush Valley, near Neath, and while he was engaged in repairing the roadway a huge stone became displaced from the side and fell on his head.

The injuries to the head were terrible, the skull being smashed, and death must have been instantaneous. The deceased man's colleagues were David John Rees and Godfrey Rees, and it appears that the three men had been working the seam, and that the formation of a company locally was under contemplation.

Deceased leaves a widow and three children.

Well-known at Swansea

Funeral of Chief Organiser of N.U.G.W.

workings to the main mine road in slides or sledges drawn by boys aged from 10 to 13 years old, using a chain passing from a girdle around the waist and between the legs to a hook on the front of the sledge. The sledges weighed approximately two hundredweight and were dragged for distances of 50 to 60 yards. The firm of Penrose and Evans in those days started children working at any age from eight to 10 years.

Eaglesbush Colliery was mentioned in a report dated 1849 on accidents in coal mines, and Henry Hussey Vivian gave evidence to the effect that prior to 1849, the Eaglesbush Colliery had no means of providing sufficient ventilation, and that: "the mine was apparently in so unsafe a state that anything would have exploded it."

An explosion did occur there early in 1848 in which 22 people were killed. Following this disaster, the owners had a ventilator installed in February 1849.

From 1854 there were many owners and the changes of name such as Penrose in 1854, Evans 1865, JB Williams 1870, the Eaglesbush Coal Co 1871, J John 1880 and the Eaglesbush Colliery Co. Limited in 1891. There were 39 people employed in 1895 and by 1900 there were 317. This figure fell to 258 early in 1903 and by the end of the year the colliery was abandoned.

In the late 19th and early 20th Century, a small handful of mines opened in the Eaglesbush Valley. They were the Treany, the Tyn-y-Coed, and the old Treany Colliery which provided coal for the Cambrian brickworks.

Also in the valley were Cryddan level and another small mine which revived the name Eaglesbush and worked the Treany Seam until abandoned in 1927.

It was September 21, 1923 at the Treany Seam that Robert Ernest Jones of Albany Terrace, Llantwit Road, formally of Whittington Street was killed. He was the grandfather of Mrs Joyce Michael of New Henry Street. His death certificate gives the cause of death as a fractured skull in an accident caused by a fall of stone. On the front page of the South Wales Daily Post, newspaper on September 22, 1923, the heading read:

'Local Collier's Terrible Death.' Her grandfather aged only 36 was working with two colleagues, brothers David and Godfrey Rees, when the accident happened. The deceased left a widow and three children.

Four years later work at the Treany Seam ended and it was abandoned.

Pictured in the late 19th Century, is a horse drawn Gipsy caravan on the open field by Albert Road and Old Furnace Terrace. A family of Gipsies used the fields as a stopover site during the year to attend the local horse fairs, that were held at Penrhiwtyn and Neath.

There would be about a dozen horses on the fields. The last time that this site was used by gipsies was around 1947. Albert Road and Old Furnace Terrace have long gone. Today Grove Lane flats, Morgan's Road and Melin Close flats are there. During the Second World War, a cabin was built to house four air raid wardens. It was located at the end of Old Furnace Terrace. Ken Chapple from Cadoxton, originally from Westbourne Road, told me that his father Dick was one of those air raid wardens, Ken, a seven year old at the time, recalls his father's uniform with the ARP badge. One of his jobs during the blackout was to ensure that no lights were showing. He remembers the air raid shelter at the bottom of Westbourne Road. When bombs fell they had a whistling noise and a job for the warden was to count the whistles and make sure the same number of bangs followed. On one occasion five fell on the Old Road, causing severe damage, but there were only four bangs, so an unexploded bomb had to be detected. Fortunately this was done without any further damage.

Bridging the gap to the Metal Box

These workmen were engaged in the construction of the Metal Box bridge over the Neath canal in 1936. The photograph belonged to Aubrey Evans from Skewen who can be seen on the right of the picture sitting on the sand. He was a 15 year old boy working for the construction firm Sir Lindsey Parkinson at the time. A few other men in the photograph are Bill Nicholas from Ethel Street, Mr. Phillips from King Street, David Davies and Mr. Harris. It was interesting to learn from Mr. Evans that he later became a good friend of Sir Harry Secombe. They both served in the Royal Artillery together and took part in the landings of North Africa, Sicily and Italy.

Neath Community Council officials, officers and members during the opening of the new Community Council Day Centre at Melyncrythan in 1990/91. They are, front row, left to right: Christine Williams, Mervyn Davies, Agnes John, Vice Chairman Sheila Penry, Chairman Dennis Curtis, Glan Pascoe and David Huckridge. Back row, left to right:Maureen Jones, George Gammon, Keith Holmes, Derek Vaughan, Gwyneth Lloyd Davies, Walter Noonan, Jack Jenkins and Huw Lewis.

The Melin Advice Centre, Briton Ferry Road was officially opened on May 1, 2004, by Edwina Hart AM. The centre is available for community use with a wide range of advice-giving agencies holding regular sessions there. The East Ward councillors also hold a monthly surgery there. Below, Leighton Andrews AM, Deputy Minister for Regeneration, officially opens the Melin Technology Centre on Thursday, June 26, 2008, watched by Charles Henry Wood, chairman of the Melyncrythan Community Conference and James Muir, the conference's treasurer.

Underneath the old oak tree

The story about this old oak tree in the Eaglesbush Valley, is an emotional and heart rending one. Sisters Beryl Jenkins of Cae Rhys Ddu Road and Betty Flynn of Wallace Road, were listening to Roy Noble on BBC Radio Wales one Sunday, when he asked if any listeners had interesting stories about trees.

This prompted Betty to write in, explaining the family's love of and interest in trees, especially one tree in particular, an oak in the Eaglesbush Valley.

Brought up in Wallace Road, Betty was one of three children. She had a sister Beryl and brother Graham. When Graham was about 10 years old, he liked to play up in the woods with his friends and one day he carved his initials into this oak tree. Graham went on to the County School, and it was here he learned a poem called Trees, which was recorded as a song by Paul Robeson and Arthur Tracey the street singer. This was a favourite song of their mother's, which she used to play when Graham was away during the war.

When Graham died in Leicester where he lived, he was 79 years old, it was planned that his family would carry out his wishes, and scatter his ashes around that old oak tree. Sadly, only three months after he died his youngest daughter Christine died, so it wasn't only Graham's ashes but Christine's too that were scattered under that tree. After hearing this story the sisters received a phone call from BBC Wales TV asking if they would be willing to be filmed for the programme 'I Love Wales.'

The TV crew arrived at Wallace Road and they were all conveyed to the Eaglesbush Valley, with which they were all impressed. The researcher for the BBC climbed the special tree, grown very large after almost 70 years, and much to the delight of everyone, the initials GR were still visible.

The programme was shown with Graham's family and his County School friend Kenneth Hopkins of Beacons View, Cimla, formerly from Jenkins Road. Kenneth was seen being interviewed by the waterfall not too far from that old tree.

The research team was successful in uncovering a copy of the old record of the Trees Song by Arthur Tracey which was played throughout the programme.

This cottage at the bottom of Foundry Road, leading to the beautiful Eaglesbush Valley, stood empty and derelict for many years before being refurbished as seen below. Houses in Bryn Road are visible on the sky line. It is a good example of how change comes about, but often slowly.

Chapter 2

Colourful characters

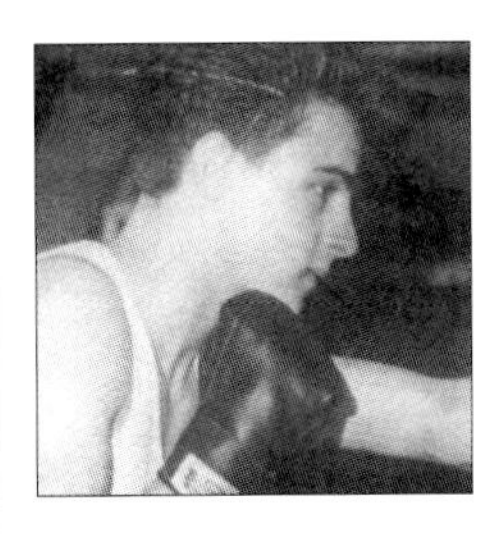

Most communities have them, those colourful characters who play such an important, yet often overlooked part in our everyday lives. The Melin is no exception and there is no doubt that down the years it has had its share. Some of them are recalled here.

William Rees Jones, for example, was a Melin man,who had a book published in 1993 called Give Us This Day, early memoirs of William Rees Jones. The title was appropriate because he was one of the great men of baking and founder of the Institute of British Bakers. In the book he recalls times from his early life in the Melin right through until his retirement in 1973.

Born in 1909 he was one of four sons of David William Jones, a carpenter and Martha Jones, who lived in Crythan Road. William attended the Melin School which to him offered the happiest days of his life, despite the disciplinarian head teacher Mr Davies who was nicknamed the Hangman.

He recalls fondly his time as a youngster playing in the Eaglesbush woods, on the rocks above Crythan Road, his Sunday school days in Marshfield Road and later at Maes-yr-haf. William Rees was one of four Melin schoolboys to pass the scholarship to the County School, which he puts down to the excellent tuition and enthusiasm inspired by the teachers at the Melin. The other three boys were Eddie Thomas, Gladstone Griffiths and Sidney Parr.

His years at the Cadoxton Road School were the most miserable of his life. He did take a particular dislike to the head teacher, when on one occasion he questioned the boys in his form on what they would like to do on leaving school, William Rees replied "Chef, Sir" which was met with roars of laughter. Little did he realise then that he would become renowned in his profession.

At the age of 15 he became apprentice to one of the best craftsman in South Wales, Fred Stockham the baker, who pointed William Rees in the right direction for his career as a baker. In 1929 when he was 20 he signed as pastry cook on the RMS Oronties on her maiden voyage. He later decided to take up bakery teaching as a career. His book goes on to tell of his first teaching post in Wrexham and his time in the Army when he served in France during the Second World War. It also tells of his many years spent at Blackpool Technical College and his work at the University

William Rees Jones - enjoyed his days at the Melin School.

City and Guilds of London Institute

SILVER MEDAL

Awarded to William Rees Jones?

First in Final Examinations 1928

Attended Melin Boys School : 1914-1920

Awarded Scholarship to Neath County School : 1920

Awarded National Scholarship to :-

Cardiff Technical College : 1925

Invented Micro Wave Oven : 1947

A glass framed certificate in Melin junior school.

College off the Gold Coast in West Africa until his retirement from business in 1973 because of his wife May's ill health. She died in 1975. In 1947 William Rees Jones developed the high frequency dielectric oven, forerunner of the microwave, working in GEC's research laboratories and demonstrating the process. At the time it was thought a useful tool for research but of no commercial value. In fact it was 20 years ahead of its time. The Melin Junior School where William Rees spent, as he is quoted as saying, 'the happiest days of his life' has two large glass framed certificates on show. One is from the City and Guilds of London with William Rees' silver medal set in and the other an award for his final exam in bread making first class, flour confectionery first class and first prize equal silver medal. A man who has fond memories of William Rees Jones is Fred Stockham who remembers him as a wonderful craftsman.

Motorbike man Harry's voyages of discovery

Harry Robathan was one of seven children born to Jack and Kate Robathan of Penrhiwtyn Street. In 1920 at the age of five he started school in Cwrt Sart, the year it first opened.

When he was 12 and still in school he used to help out in John Baskerville's garage by serving petrol until, in 1931, as a 16 year old he began work in the Galv works and remained there for 27 years until 1958.

It was from the Galv as a 17 year old that Harry was chosen to attend the Duke of York Camp in Suffolk in 1933. This was set up by the Duke of York, later to become King George VI, for boys in various industries and boys in public schools. Around 400 youngsters from all parts of the country attended. Two 17 year olds were chosen from the Galv works, Harry being one and Harold Thomas, the former Neath and Wales second row, who signed for Salford in 1937 the other. Two other young men who accompanied them were Ernie Bentley from Florence Street and Ewart Cottell from Briton Ferry.

A giant marquee in the camp called the Duke of York Theatre, showed films and slides. It was here that the famous Lord Clydesdale personally showed slides of when he made the first Everest flight in 1933. Harry recalled that the Duke of York gave out photographs of himself signed simply, Albert. He later became King George VI, Queen Elizabeth II father. He would have been King Albert, only due to a promise by the family to Queen Victoria that no future King would take the name of her beloved Albert.

From the Galv Harry went to the Abbey Works until he retired in 1976. His two passions in life were motorbikes and ships. He had his first bike in 1940. The previous owner was councillor Jenkins of Coronation Road. Harry used to take part in motorcycle scrambles, and rode until 1998 when he was then 82 years old. His love of ships had been with him since he was a young lad. He wanted to the Royal Navy but his father refused.

Over the years he enjoyed 12 cruises and there is nothing he didn't know about the ill-fated Titanic. He even corresponded with one of the survivors of the disaster, Eva Hart and had a picture signed by her. Harry's interest in the Titanic spans much longer than most of us because it was only in the last few years of the 20th century that general interest was aroused when the wreck of the ship was found after 80 years at the bottom of the sea and later, of course, the blockbuster film Titanic which caused such a stir was released.

Harry had an old newspaper in his possession. It was a special edition, in memory of Titanic, of the Daily Telegraph, dated April 20, 1912. Priced at one penny this was produced just six days after the Titanic struck the iceberg and sunk on Sunday April 14. The paper shows the unbelievable splendour of the first class passenger suites, the Georgian Smoke Room panelled in the finest mahogany, the swimming pool, Turkish baths and the main staircase from the great hall.

The newspaper contains a photograph of Captain Smith standing alongside the Titanic on the day of its departure from Southampton on April 10. There is also a photo of John Philips (Jack) the wireless operator whose SOS signal was received by ocean-going liners hundreds of miles away. There are many photos of survivors along with their harrowing stories. One of those was Eva Hart, with whom Harry corresponded with a number of times. Eva was a young girl of seven emigrating to America with her parents Benjamin and Esther Hart. They were second class passengers and their ticket number was 13529. It had cost them just over £26. Eva and her mother were picked up by the vessel Carpathia.

Harry Robathan of Brookdale Street, on his first beloved motorbike on Aberavon beach in 1942 during the Second World War.

The picture of the Titanic signed by survivor Eva Hart that Harry Robathan cherished.

Benny Grant

Benny Grant was a legend in the Melin. He devoted more than 65 years of his life to encouraging youngsters in the area to take up boxing. He was only 16 years old when he opened his first gym in Eva Street. Eventually a series of others followed at various locations throughout Neath. The last was in Rockfield Terrace which sadly burned down in 1994. Benny was employed in the Melin Tinplate Works. When War broke out he wasn't accepted in the armed forces because of his disability so he joined the Territorial Army and was stationed in Usk. Benny even won a boxing medal in the Army when he beat a corporal in the Royal Hussars. A final accolade for him came in 1994 when he received a High Sheriff 's award for his services to the Community. Benny and his devoted wife Mary celebrated their Diamond Wedding in 1999.

Benny Grant with Ivor Evans at a training session at Marshfield Road gym in the 1950s.

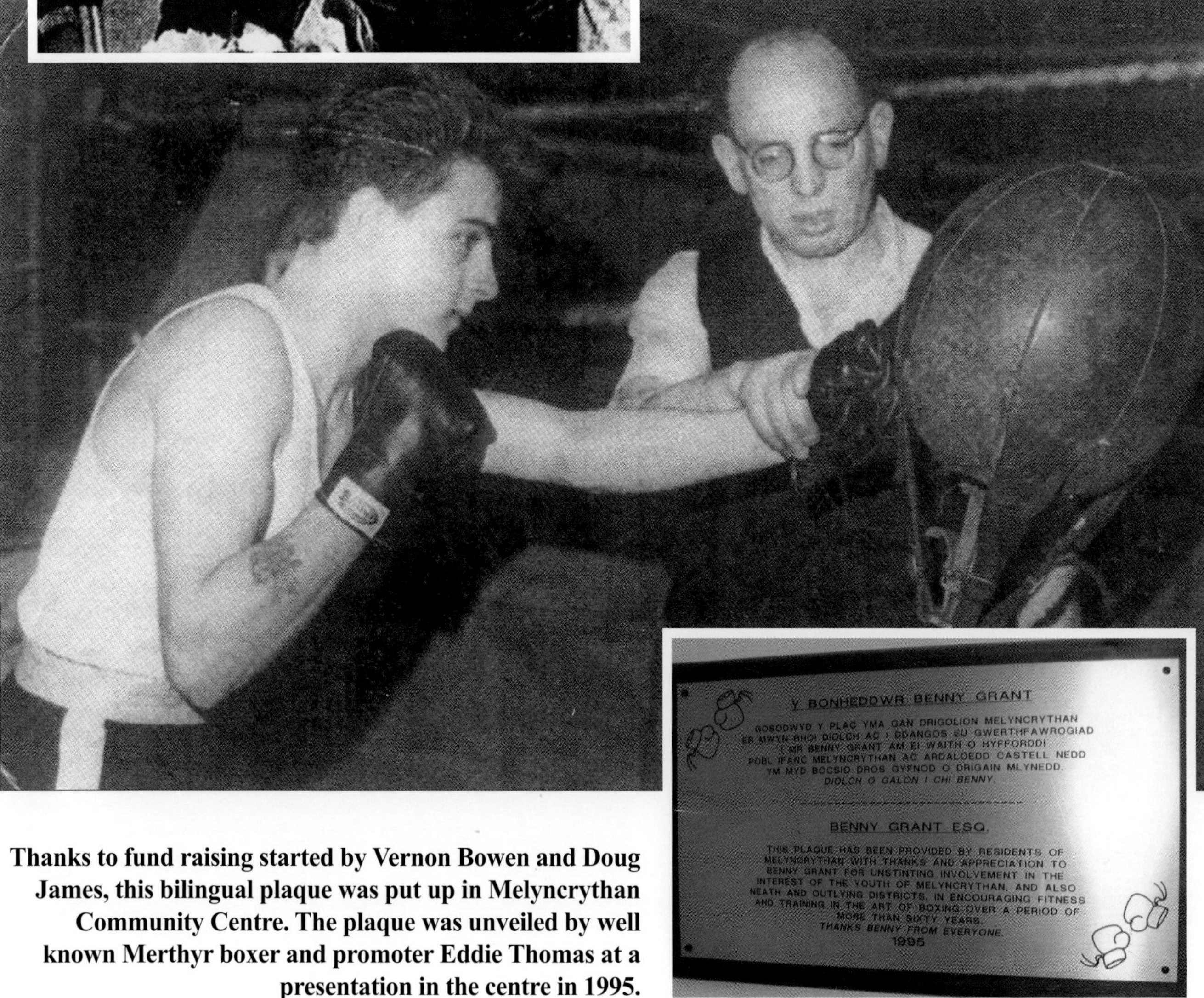

Thanks to fund raising started by Vernon Bowen and Doug James, this bilingual plaque was put up in Melyncrythan Community Centre. The plaque was unveiled by well known Merthyr boxer and promoter Eddie Thomas at a presentation in the centre in 1995.

Two young lads who left to find their fortune

Down the years many Melin people have found themselves in interesting situations. One in particular was Tom Jones who became a personal body guard to Sir Winston Churchill.

Seeing the photograph above of the Melin's Farmers Arms senior citizen patrons taken in 1950, prompted a telephone call from Tom, who by this time had moved to Northumberland. He had been sent a copy of it by his sister Megan. Tom's father, Tom Jones of Mountain Ash, after whom he was named, is one of those in the picture. Tom was born in Payne Street, as were his sisters, Megan and Glenys. As a youngster he was a pupil of the Melin School.

At the age of 17, he and a pal from Hillside, Tommy Bowen, left the Melin to seek their fortune in England. They both ended up joining the Welsh Guards in 1930, where Tom remained until 1937 at which point he joined the police in London. When war came he was called up and became a sergeant in the Welsh Guards. That's when, for a time, he became a personal guard to Winston Churchill at 10 Downing Street. Later he was also one of the guards when Churchill was lying in state. During the wartime blitz on London he was seriously wounded and spent many months in hospital in Hertfordshire. In 1944, one of his fellow patients was Peter Ustinov, who at that time was just starting out on his illustrious acting career. After the war Tom continued his career in the police and for a number of years he and his wife and three sons lived in Australia, carrying on his career as a policeman. Back in England he later worked for the Ministry of Defence, until he retired at the age of 74. What tales he has to tell of those years since he left Payne Street. For him seeing this old photo touched his heart and rekindled memories of his younger days in the Melin.

Included in the picture above are: Farmers Arms patrons Sid Williams (Squib), George Clarke, Olga Clarke, Dai Lloyd, Kae James (Crynant), Joe Richards (Comedian), Willie Jenkins, George Clarke Snr, Tom Jones (Mountain Ash), Ted Allen (Crynant), Tom Charles, Jack Rees, Jim Dumphey, Dai Emanuel, Edmond Mathews (Major), Alex Francis, Ernie Parsons and Hywel Jenkins.

Taken during the First World War, this photograph was loaned by Moira Wiggins. It shows the Morgan family who had a bicycle shop in Briton Ferry Road.

Thomas Morgan is seen seated with his wife leaning on his shoulder, with nine of his children. Seated next to him is his daughter, Martha, Moira's mother. Seated on the other end is Hilda J Davies, a well known Neath music teacher and for many years musical director of the Melincrythan Amateur Operatic Society. The officer on the left in the photograph is Ivor Morgan, of Lewis Road, a local businessman. At the back is David L. Morgan, a vocal teacher in Briton Ferry. The young boy at the front is Morgan Morgan. During the war Thomas Morgan and his wife often entertained 'walking wounded' soldiers in their home at their cycle shop in Briton Ferry Road.

The servicemen were from nearby Penrhiwtyn hospital. Thomas Morgan was the first man in Neath to own a motorbike and he once rode from Land's End to John O' Groats in Scotland.

Morgan Morgan at his 100th birthday celebration in 2006 with his nieces Moira Wiggins from Lewis Road and Connie Ommanney from Cadoxton.

Joe Richards

Joe Richards was a well known comedian and character in the Neath area. He was born in Ethel Street and was a friend of Ernie Speed another local entertainer. He was the youngest of six children born to Joseph and Matilda Richards. There was Liza Ann, Elizabeth, Maud, Samuel, Francis, who was killed in First World War, aged just 19 and Joe who was born in 1904. Joe was in ENSA and performed on the popular radio show Welsh Rarebit. He was also in panto and appeared at the Grand Theatre Swansea where a handbill described him as a comedian and step dancer. Joe had also worked at Vint's Picture Palace which was on the site of Neath Post Office in Windsor Road. After Joe married he lived in Old Henry Street. Locally he was well known in the Farmers Arms and Paddy's Club where he played the drums and entertained. Many of his family have followed in his footsteps. His nephew Roy was a talented musician who many will remember playing the organ and accordion, his nephew David played the trumpet and Joe's great nephew Alan, took over from him on the drums in Paddy's Club.

Ernie Speed

Ernie Speed seen here dressed as Burlington Bertie was a postman who travelled the country as an entertainer. Ernie had a brother Will who lived next to the Eaglesbush Pub. During the First World War in 1915 Will came to Neath to work on the railway. He was a fireman and later an engine driver. He married May Griffiths from the Melin.

Ernie served in the First World War and was seriously wounded. He was shot in the arm and he also lost an eye. At that time Neath Infirmary at Penrhiwtyn had been turned into a military hospital and it was here that Ernie was sent. It was a coincidence that his brother lived so near in the Melin. Ernie went on to marry another Griffiths sister Ellen. So the two brothers ended up married to two sisters. Ernie and Ellen lived in Helen's Road.

One lasting memory for Dave Williams of Port Talbot regarding his uncle Ernie was that every night he used to take out his glass eye, polish it and put it in his trouser pocket. David often asked him why he did that. His answer was to keep an eye on his money so that his Aunty Ellen didn't have it.

Brian and Mary Harris

Brian and Mary Harris from Stoke on Trent on the occasion of their Golden Wedding. They were married in St John's Church, Skewen in 1955. Brian was born in Crythan Road, Melin and Mary in Crymlyn Road, Skewen. Brian, was the only one out of 135 Melin School pupils to win a place to Neath Grammar School in 1945. His Christian ethics were nurtured by his old Sunday school teacher at St Catherine's Church, William Challacombe, a former Mayor of Neath. Brian started work in 1949, as office messenger at the Eaglesbush Tinplate Works, Melin, progressing through several departments before being called up for National Service at the age of 18.

On his return from active service in Egypt and Kenya he rejoined the staff at the Eaglesbush Works in January 1955. Later that year he started work with Cow and Gate Limited in Guildford and a few years later in 1960 he joined Revlon International at its factory in Maesteg, as financial accountant. Its rapid expansion led to him being appointed financial controller of the company's Irish operation in Dublin. He continued with Revlon and became financial controller for Europe in 1970. In 1973 Brian accepted an invitation to join the Max Factor cosmetics company.

Brian and Mary Harris

Since retiring in 1998 Brian has pursued his hobby of writing poetry about his oversees visits, in the 1970s and 1980s with Max Factor. When in South Africa, it was through one of his poems that he struck up a relationship with the former President Nelson Mandela. Their correspondence started with James Gregory, who was his jailer for 18 years, mainly on Robben Island. Nelson Mandela has framed copies of two poems Brian wrote in Capetown in 1979 when he sat opposite Robben Island across the Bay.

In 1997 Brian was invited to Washington DC by the International Society of Poets in Maryland to be inaugurated as the International Poet of Merit at their annual convention. It was in 2003 Brian received the Military General Service Medal awarded to those who served on the Suez Canal, during the emergency between 1951 and 1954. He was also posted to Khartoum, Sudan, Nairobi and Kenya for service in the Mau Mau uprising. Brian's first news of the award came from a former MP and well known television presenter Sir Geoffrey Johnston-Smith, an old friend. Sir Geoffrey retired from Parliament in 1997. Brian and Mary have been living in Stoke-On-Trent for many years, but Wales they said will forever remain in their hearts.

Bertie Mellin

Bertie Mellin was born in Ethel Street. He worked for years in the sheet mills at the Galv. He was known as the toughest man in Neath and took part in many bare knuckle fights in different pubs in the valleys, walking to the venues sometimes over the mountains from one valley to another and then back home. He was managed by his mother who used to train him by making him drag a horse cart back and fore over the old Galv tip.

It was in late November 1932 that the great boxer Tommy Farr faced Bertie Mellin of Neath at Pontarddulais. Tommy boxed with great caution to take a 10 round decision. At this time Tommy Farr was 20 years old and not a fully fledged heavyweight. So the man of courage from the Melin had fought a great fighter who was later to box the great Joe Louis for the World Championship.

In later years Bertie's last job was for Ken Richards the undertaker where he looked after the limousines and he was often seen on the coldest of days washing the cars down, the water freezing, no coat on and shirt sleeves rolled up. He was as hard as nails, but someone who, it is said, had a heart of gold.

William Bowen, 1906 - 1988.

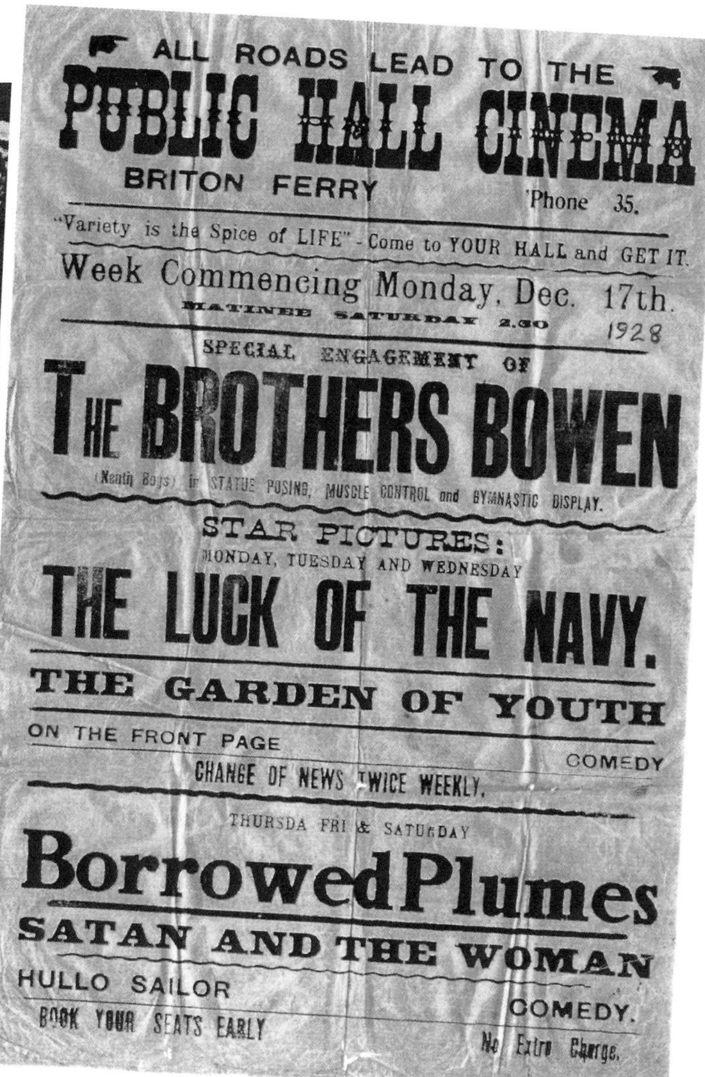

The Brothers Bowen

Brothers Harold and Willie Bowen were born in Howells Street, now Danygraig Road, sons of Morgan and Magdalene Bowen. Morgan, a miner, died while sinking a pit in Burry Port. His sons followed in his footsteps and worked as miners too. Harold began his working life in Cefn Coed Colliery at the age of nine.

The year 1926 brought the famous General Strike and it was at that time that brothers Harold and Willie decided to do something with themselves and went along to the White Hart Pub in Neath where the Landlord Tommy Bates had a gym in an upstairs room. There they learned everything there was to know regarding fitness and muscle control and put together a programme of their acrobatic and gymnastic skills, thus forming an act they called the Brothers Bowen. They ended up as semi-professionals and for about seven years performed in venues such as the Swansea Empire, The Palace in Neath, Gnoll Hall, St Catherine's Hall and The Public Hall Cinema, Briton Ferry. Willie then left Neath to look for work in Cornwall, which he found, and he married a Cornishwoman and had a daughter Joan. Harold meanwhile went on to work in the Galv where he was known by his nickname Cowboy. He served in the Army during the Second World War. He lived in New Henry Street with his family and continued working at the Galv until he retired at the age of 65.

Harold Bowen, 1902-1990.

Captain Routledge

Captain Alexander Ancel Routledge, right who lived from 1818 to 1902 was a master mariner and inventor who was the great grandfather of Bill Adams of Cimla Common. Captain Routledge invented the Emigrant's lifebelt. In the mid 19th Century loss of life at sea was very heavy, so Captain Routledge with his experience at sea and his inventive mind designed and constructed a lifebelt at his workshop in Neath. He was so confident that it would work successfully that he demonstrated the lifebelt himself by jumping into the sea at Ilfracombe. Captain Routledge also invented the detonator that was used extensively as a fog signal on Britain's railways. He lived in Briton Ferry Road, next to the Royal Exchange Inn and served as a Ratepayer councillor on Neath Borough Council for three years. Captain Routledge was also Neath Harbour commissioner in 1884.

Nelson Napier Routledge, son of Captain AA Routledge of Briton Ferry Road with his wife Elizabeth, daughter of David Thomas, Station Master Neath from 1852 – 1882.

Captain AA Routledge and, below, a bill heading from the turn of the 20th Century for Coal Merchant Nelson Routledge. The depot was in Exchange Road and the entrance can still be seen.

BEST COALS BEST COALS BEST COALS

MELINCRYTHAN, NEATH.

191

M

Bot. of NELSON ROUTLEDGE,

Coal Merchant.

Best Large and other House Coals at Lowest Possible Prices.

Date Tons Cwts Qrs. Description Rate £ s.

Bill Cotton

Bill Cotton served the Melin community as Borough and later County Borough councillor for 27 years. He was first elected to Neath Borough Council in 1972 as a representative for Neath South. He was Mayor of Neath in 1982-83 and chairman of the council's planning committee. He was a very popular character in the town. Bill was born in Gasworks Road in August 1914. He went to Melin School and his first job was with the Post Office. Later he became a labourer with the South Wales Electricity Board and finally moved into the office, eventually becoming its Neath shop manager. For 40 years he was secretary, chairman and a committee man of the Mackworth Club in Windsor Road,. His devoted work with the Trade Union movement, Neath Trades Council and Clubs Institute Union was unstinting. He was also a faithful member of New Maria Congregational Church. Bill and his wife Edna celebrated their diamond wedding in 1999.

Mrs Annie Langham celebrates her 100th birthday at a party with Neath Ladies Pensioners group. Pictured with Annie are Beryl Hutchings, Nancy Evans, Doreen Sparkes, Joan Pike, Rita Nicholas, Blanche Phillips, Audrey Harris, Mary Gunter and Dorothy Jones, Annie was born in 1904 at 1 Edward Street. She worked in the Metal Box Factory during and after the Second World War. When she married husband Michael they lived in Evans Road and later moved to Morgans Road.

Phyllis Mogford of Old Road celebrating her 100th birthday with her sister May and members of the Neath Ladies Pensioners. A lifelong Melin woman, Phyllis was born in School Road in 1904. Her father George Henry Mogford was chief engineer in the Galv. Phyllis, who attended Herbert Road School, played tennis, badminton and cricket, which she played on her grandfather's field in Gardeners Lane which is a housing estate now. She was also a talented hockey player and became a member of the South Wales team. If war hadn't broken out she would probably have played for Wales. After her schooldays she took over the family grocery business on the corner of School Road and Old Road. She ran it for about 22 years before eventually moving to the Old Road. She was a staunch member of St Catherine's Church, the Ladies Pensioners and Mothers Union group's there. Pictured are: Beryl Hutchings, chairwoman; Nancy Evans, secretary; Rita Nicholas, Sheila Penry, Doreen Sparkes, Glenys Newbury, Florrie Jenkins and Audrey Harris.

John Gorman

Successful businessman John Gorman, the owner of Gorman Glass, in Windsor Road started his business from his home in Penrhiwtyn Street. He had served an apprenticeship as a glazier with Vernon Thomas of Briton Ferry. Because he was unable to get suitable premises John transferred his business to Pontardawe. It was in September 1969 that he moved back to Neath and opened his shop in Windsor Road. After a number of years he finally moved to the firm's present site near Stockhams Corner. As well as carrying on his trade as a glazing contractor, he specialised in selling a wide variety of glassware. Mr Gorman's son Andrew runs the business today. The Gorman Glass Shop at Stockhams Corner for many years boasted a host of illuminated decorations in the run up to Christmas as the pictures below show. It was always a wonderful display and the shop won Neath town's best Christmas window display for a number of years.

Les Treharne

Les Treharne of Eastland Road started his working life in the pay office of the Galv. When the war came in 1939, he joined the RAF and served in the Middle East. He was later section superintendent with the Prudential Insurance company and district manager with Scottish Legal Assurance until he retired. Les was well known for his work in the Scout movement. He started as a young Cub and worked his way to King Scout, receiving every honour in the movement. He was founder member of 3rd Neath troop where he had been a leader. When Les retired in the 1970s he took up bowls and represented the county on numerous occasions. He was a founder member of Neath RAFA Club, former president of Neath Pensioners Association and one of the oldest members of St David's Church.

Adrian Pickerell

Former Melin boy Adrian Pickerell is now living in Germany. Born in 1965, he is the son of Gaynor and Tony Pickerell, the former Cardiff City and Wales footballer. He attended The Melin School and Cwrt Sart Comprehensive. After leaving there in 1982 he joined the Royal Air Force, serving at home and finally Germany. He then volunteered for a commando course and eventually transferred to the Army, serving in the Royal Hussars. He stayed in Germany because he had found a decent job there in the beautiful town of Munster. He met Petra, a German nurse in 1997 and they married in 2007. They have one son Adam. Since 2002 he has been drawing weekly comic strips and editorial cartoons for two newspapers, as well as writing and illustrating diverse magazines and journals. He is fluent in German both written and spoken. Adrian spends a great deal of time writing stories about Neath and the Melin, something he enjoys very much because it serves as a bridge to his roots and a very happy childhood at home and in the Melin and Cwrt Sart Schools. A poem he has written called The Melin Brook tells the games he played in the Melin woods back in the days when imaginations ran wild.

The Melin brook

This is a poem about the Melin brook
that runs through the woods where we stopped to look,
back in the days when our world was small
and games of adventure were most important of all.
we played out scenes from film and book
and our screen and stage was the Melin brook

There where the brook rounds a rocky bend
we fought the Zulu's to the bitter end,
and how often from Red Indians I ran
as the last surviving cavalryman
and there where the leaves adorn a crooked tree
the leading lady was saved by me.

When our parents called at the end of the day
with hungry bellies we went away
for an evening meal and then a film or book
to be played out tomorrow at the Melin brook.
At night I'd dream the whole night through
Of doing things that heroes do.

Nowadays or so it seems
the children are fixed to their computer screens
they never seem to leave the house
imagination replaced by the click of a mouse.
That's progress they say and my head it shook
As my thoughts returned, to the Melin brook.

Len Palfry

Len Palfry was born and brought up in Old Henry Street and when he married he moved to Herbert Road and then in 1954 to Meadow Road. Len worked in the Eaglesbush Tinplate works for 45 years until retirement. He was a keen skittles player and was still playing for the Royal Exchange inn at the age of 87. He started playing for the Eaglesbush pub in 1935 ad this was the start of an association with the Neath and District Skittles League that spanned more than 70 years. During that time he became its chariman and card secretary. Len has a wonderful memory and is a mine of information on all things to do with the Melin.

Blanche Hurn

Blanche Hurn of Old Road was born Blanche Dickinson in Mile End Row and she has written down her memories of growing up in the 1930s in the Melin. They include recollections of the time she attended Herbert Road School. Although she only lived a few doors from the Melin School, it was overcrowded. At that time the games they played were whip and top, skipping and hop scotch. The times they had flooding in Mile End Row were something to remember. If it rained for a long time her mother would go upstairs. If the tide was out they were safe, if not the carpet in the front room would come up and furniture would be taken upstairs. In the 1930s the Melin was quite an interesting place to be. It was home to the Japan Works, Galv, Eagle, the building of the Metal Box, and also a variety of shops. It was the Co-op where most people shopped, for that little bit of dividend. The Melin had plenty of pubs, eight up to the Exeter. Then there were the Creek brothers, Henry, Billy and Dai. They brought their horse and cart around with rabbits at 6d and 9d hanging from a canopy. Rabbit pie and stew were a favourite then. Blanche's wonderful memories go on and on.

A number of Melin faces can be seen in the crowd that gathered outside the Gwyn Hall, Neath, in 1979, during a visit there from former Prime Minister Edward Heath.

Anita Williams

One Christmas tradition has not changed for Anita Williams from Kingdon Owen Road, formally from Mile End Row. She still has the tree her Mum, Edith Pike, bought in 1943. This attracted media attention when the story not only appeared in local newspapers but also in many daily newspapers. The tree was bought when the family lived in Mile End Row in the Melin. Anita was only five years old. She even has the original box it was in. Anita recalls that at that time the country was in the midst of the Second World War. That year 27 Allied merchant vessels were sunk by German U-boats in just four days. It was in that battle of the Atlantic that her brother lost his life. He was Edward Pike, a chef, serving on the SS Pelus when it was sunk by a U-boat. He managed to get into a raft with some of his shipmates, but was shot by the Germans. He was only 21 years of age. His name is on the memorial gates at the Gnoll, and also on a plaque in St Catherine's Church. Anita said it was a dreadful day in 1943 when her mother received the telegram telling of her beloved son's death. As they say life goes on and for Anita this tree will always be a reminder of her mother and brother from way back in that year of 1943.

Song of the Melin

What wonderous tales I have been told, of the Melin in the days of old.
Of Annie Nick-Nock, Rastus too, who slit his throat in the outside loo.
My Auntie, who was only three, called to ask if she could see.

Walls whitewashed to kill the bugs, floors, scrubbed white and handmade rugs.
Black leaded grate where coal fire glowed, a clock to wind, in case it slowed.
Tin-bath hanging on a nail, used each night without fail.

Girls play skipping in the street, ribbons tied so nice and neat.
Boys skinning knees in rough old games, chasing, shouting, down the lanes.
"Don't tell that I pulled your hair, come on let's play kiss and dare."

Men who toiled in the Rolling Mill, sweated pints and drank their fill.
Ladies standing top of street, charging sixpence for a treat.
Maggie Liz and Sarah Jayne, one good as gold, one full of shame.

Old women in the bottle or jug, or sipping stout in the Snug.
Wearing men's caps, hair in a bun. Our men have gone to Paddies for fun.
Get back to give the fire a poke, we know the men will come home broke.

A Melin bride, a joy to see, groom throws coppers for you and me.
A ribbon stretched across the door, a leap brings luck forever more.
Do not push the silk aside, or one day you will lose your bride.

A Melin death, everyone mourned, curtains drawn tightly, black was loaned.
Neighbours gather their friends who weep, memories aired for all to keep.
The coffin's here, take off your hat, the ladies in the parlour sat.

Does the Melin still exist? I don't know but I'll tell you this.
As long as their children are alive, the song of the Melin will survive.
What wonderous tales I have been told, of the Melin in the days of old.

The children grow too old for toys, and go to school at Melin boys.
With Melin girl's school by the side, and school motto carved with pride.
"Manners maketh man" it states, be kind, be good to all classmates.

Two schools divided by a wall, but they shared the dinner hall.
Across the yard the boys would stride, the girls would all pretend to hide.
But now and then a nod, a wink, today it's you I love, I think.

Saturday picnics up the "Cwm" stumbling back down Stoney Road home.
Chapel vestry for Sunday School, a verse to remember was the rule.
Then arm in arm, all troubles fade, a walk around Monkies Parade.

Elaine Rowlands

Elaine Rowlands, a renowned local poet has had many of her poems published. She was born in 1937 in Old Road, and lived most of her early life in Coronation Road. She attended Melin School and at 14 moved to Slough. She lived in various parts of England until 1969, when she emigrated to Australia with her parents and two children. She returned three years later, leaving her parents in Australia and lived with her grandmother in Coronation Road until housed in Burnside where she lived until she married Ron Rowlands in 1985 and moved to Tonna.
The first poem she had published was in a Welsh Anthology in 1994. More publications followed, but she found she was unable to write after the death of her husband in 2000. She decided to return to writing after the encouragement she received when her poem The Ivy Tower was displayed in the School and Rugby Club in Tonna. Elaine is one of the Cancer Challenge Singers and the Cancer Charity benefited from the sale of her books. One of Elaine's poems, about her childhood, The Song of the Melin, appears alongside.

Ronnie Williams

Jean Richards formally of Burrows Road, now living in Caerphilly brought me some information about her cousin Ronnie Williams and also a poem written by Ronnie's nephew John Campbell, a noted Belfast author. As a youngster Ronnie lived in Jenkins Road and attended the Melin School. As a teenager he worked in the Eaglesbush Works. He joined the Royal Navy at the outbreak of the Second World War and was torpedoed twice by the same U-boat and was in the freezing water for 12 hours. When asked how they stayed awake, he replied, that they sang Welsh songs. After the war he settled in Belfast with his bride Marian. Ronnie's grandparents were Mr and Mrs David and Elizabeth Emmanuel of Burrows Road, caretakers of St Catherine's Church and Parish Hall. He was one of five children born to Mr and Mrs Winifred Williams. John Campbell's poem Sailorman is dedicated to Ronnie Williams, a modest hero, like many others, to whom we owe a debt we cannot repay.

Sailorman

Sailorman, you fought for your country, well aware of
the danger it would pose.
You defended our islands with other men of courage.
Men of the Shamrock, the thistle, leek and rose.

You signed on to fight the foe in Britain's
Grim and dark days.
When Britain stood alone, as Hitler burned
and bombed and slaughtered.
On the oceans of the world you helped destroy
the Axis Forces.
From Dunkirk up to Iceland with
your pennant holed and tattered.

Sometime in the forties, your ship pulled into Belfast.
There you received some shore leave
to rest you from the strife.
In the district known as Dockland,
you found yourself a sweetheart.
When you returned to battle,
you and she were man and wife.

Torpedoes from the u-boats
in the freezing north Atlantic.
Cut the fleet to pieces and your ship was blown away.
Another vessel rescued you, but, too, was torpedoed.
Two ships were shot from under you,
in the space of just one day.
Your wife received the grim news
that in battle you were missing.
Admiral Donitz and his wolf packs gave our
Navy quite a licking.
But the Welsh blood that flowed through
you was the blood of kings and heroes.
And your family were informed that
you were still alive and kicking.

You joined another ship and once again
engaged in warfare.
And there you stayed until the war itself was won.
Then you swapped the valleys
for a dockside street in Belfast.
Worked in its sprawling shipyard,
sired a daughter and a son.

Sailorman, you are old now and
don't talk about your exploits.
Or the bravery that won the medals
pinned upon your chest.
I'm sure you often think about your
brave young mates who perished.

Percy Chambers

Percy Chambers was born in 1918 in Dalton Road when it was called Coronation Road and brought up in Pendrill Street. In 1933, aged just 15, he started work underground at Seven Sisters Colliery. When he married his wife Freda they moved to Danygraig Road. He joined the Army in 1940 and saw service in Italy, France, Germany, Holland and Belgium. He was demobbed in 1946. He then worked for N & C Luxury Coaches until 1951, when he joined a local insurance company, becoming manager in 1966 a post he held until he retired in 1983.

For many years Percy was involved with the Scout movement. He was secretary for Neath and District Scout Association, and for 10 years, secretary of the Welsh Scout Council. He received the highest accolade – the silver acorn – for his dedication and service to the movement.

It was in 1978 that a group of men at the Melin Social Club, guided by Robert Davies, the first chairman, and Bernard Payne the first secretary, decided to form The Melyncrythan Choir. Their first rehearsal was on Friday, October 13. No longer flying the Melyncrythan banner it changed to Neath Choir in the year 2000.

Terry Hetherington

Terry Hetherington was born in Danygraig Road in 1935. He was a labourer for most of his working life. He had been a miner, metalworker, a navvy and a builder. It wasn't until ill health and injury forced him into premature retirement in the early 1980s that he developed as a poet. For three decades Terry Hetherington has been a distinctive voice not only in the Welsh magazines but in poetry readings throughout the land and he was a very popular character on the Welsh literacy scene. He was also a member of the Owain Glyndwr Society.

A special issue of the Seventh Quarry paid tribute to Terry in their poetry magazine with poems dedicated to him by his beloved partner Aida and other prominent Welsh poets. Seventh Quarry is an international magazine that had translated and published Terry's poetry in Romania. When Terry passed away in 2007 a bursary was set up in his memory for young writers aged 16-23. A seat was designated to him outside the Dylan Thomas Centre in Swansea, a fitting tribute to such a renowned writer.

CHARLES HENRYWOOD

Charles Henrywood served as a councillor for the East Ward for 25 years. For five of those he was leader of Neath Borough Council and Mayor of the Borough of Neath in 1994/95. He was the instigator of the successful May Day in Melin Festival, Chairman of Melincryddan Community Conference and a member of the Neath East Communities First Partnership. To mark Volunteers Week in 2008, Charles was presented with a certificate by the Deputy Minister and Neath East Assembly Member, Gwenda Thomas. The certificate assigned by the first Minister Rhodri Morgan refers to Charles' work with the MCC and reads: "This certificate acknowledges the outstanding contribution made by Charles Henrywood as a volunteer with the Melincrythan Community Conference." Charles is also involved in a wide range of other voluntary activities in the community. He is also warden at St. Catherine's Church and President of Neath Male Voice Choir.

Tom James

Tom James of New Henry Street stands proudly between his Bird of Paradise and prize winning cactus plant. His daughter brought the Bird of Paradise plant from abroad when it was just a matter of inches in length and hasn't stopped growing since. Tom was born in 1910 in the family home in New Henry Street. During the war he worked in the Georgie Kent factory in Resolven and later at the Abbey Steelworks in Port Talbot until he retired. Tom loved his garden and in his younger days he also used to breed and show Welsh Terriers.

Hilary Dredge

Hilary Dredge now living in Newcastle is formally from Meadow Road. Born in 1946, the daughter of Granville and Beatrice Bunston, Hilary suffered from cerebral palsy and at the age of four was sent to a school in Devon. Despite her disability she passed the 11-plus exam and went to Grammar School, later gaining five O- levels. Hilary is married to Roy, her childhood sweetheart, who is also disabled. Prior to her marriage to Roy and moving to Newcastle, Hilary worked for 25 years at the Thomas Thomas warehouse in Swansea. In recent years Hilary was the recipient of a National Training Award, which she received for her work with a disabled group in Newcastle, called Skills for People. She visited many schools, bringing to the attention of the schoolchildren people with disabilities, and getting them to understand their problems. There were more than 300 applicants for this award, with only 23 winners. Hilary went on to receive her award greeted by lots of applause. Hilary has strength of character, independence and a sense of humour. She attributes this to her parents who brought her up to think she could do anything she put her mind to. She had a poem published called Our House which is a recollection of her home in Meadow Road.

Chapter 3

School report

School days, or so the saying goes, are among the happiest of our lives. Perhaps some would disagree with that, but there will be many with pleasant memories of their days sat behind desks in the schools that have educated local children.

Among these was the old Melin School which was built in 1873. The sketch below shows it shortly after completion in March, 1874. The school was built for the use of the work people at the Melin Tinplate Works at the sole expense of Messrs Leach, Flower & Co, the spirited proprietors of these works. Separate classrooms were provided for girls and boys. A library and reading room was attached to the school for the free use of the people employed at the works and was available for club meetings, lectures and other entertainments. The architect was Mr. Norton of London, who also designed St David's Church in Neath. The Melin School motto is Manners Maketh Man which was adopted from Winchester School where the proprietor of the tinplate works, Mr. Flower, had been a pupil.

Melin School many years after it opened. Now, an extension can be seen to the right of the building and extra windows added to the left hand side.

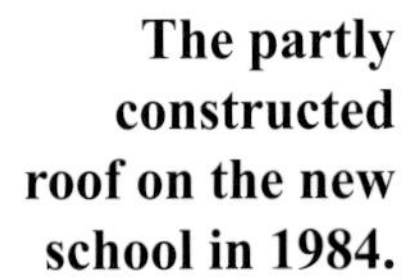

The partly constructed roof on the new school in 1984.

The new Melin School building which offered its pupils improved facilities, 1984.

These are some of the pupils who attended the Melin School in 1884. The teacher was Margaret Thomas, the daughter of David Thomas the station master at Neath. Margaret was born in 1862 and died without marrying in 1931. She was one of 13 children born to David and Martha Thomas. They lived at Whitehouse, where the Metal Box is today and later at Idris Villa, Old Road, Pencaerau. I recall saying that this photograph probably dated too far back for anyone to be recognised. I was wrong, someone was spotted. Peter Brambley of Mile End Row informed me that his grandmother was one of those Melin pupils. Her name was Suzanna Adams and she was born in Bowen Street in 1878. Also in the photograph are her brother David Adams and sister Elizabeth Adams.

Pupils of Melin Infants School, 1902. Some of them are: back row, left to right: John Harris, Johnny Francis, J Harris, David Harris, Stanley Jones. Second row: Mary Lizi, Mrs. Morgan, known to many as 'the lawyer', Dorothy Morgan, Johnny Williams, Llewellyn Williams, Gwyn Morgan, Aaron Davies, Os Moses, George Roberts, Miss Prothero, teacher. Third row: Joe Morgan, Ivor Morgan, Tillie Morgan, Florrie Jenkins. Front: Bill Dargavel, Cliff Thornton and Syd Slee.

Class 2 at Herbert Road Infants School, 1925. Among them are: Betty Thomas, Caenwen Jones, Frances Hancock, Phyllis Beddoe, Maisie Bernard, Evelyn Jones, Irene Bowen, Philip Larcombe, Megan Isaac, Betty Thomas, Iris Lewis, Harold Hudson, Danny Vaughan, Jack Davies, Ken Harries, Gwyn Williams, Bertie Ellis, Felix Crossland, Merlin Jones, Freddie Allen, Gordon Webb and Lemmie Richards.

Standard 4, Herbert Road Council School 1925. Some of the girls are: Phyllis Hardwick, Ida Dyer, Vera Jones, May Thomas, Annie Chapple, Violet Thomas, Ethel Cahn, Rosa Wright, Edna Herbert, Flossie Hodge, Norah Baker, Violet Lewis, Nellie Pearn, Maggie Powell, Annie Martin, Jenny Vaughan, Anita Hargest, Lily Cahn, Evelyn Rice, Betty Curtis, Gladys Colwill, Lynda John, Margaret Shipton, Olwen Harvard, Ivy (Surname unknown) and the teacher, Miss Brewer.

The Herbert Road Infants class in 1929. The photograph is from Blanche Hurn, who is actually among the girls. She was Blanche Dickenson then. Among the girls are: Dora Snow, Ray Amphlett, Alma Hughes, Avril Parfitt, Beryl Davies, Doris Thomas, Alma Edwards, Alberta Cole, Peggy Green, Rosalind Jenkins, Alma Richards, Rita Davies, Gwyneth Davies, Marjorie Hughes, Joan Edwards, Sheila John, Betty Huxtable, Maisie Price, Peggy Sly and Ruby Roberts. The boys are Vernon Howells, John Davies, Billy Thomas, Emanuel Harrison, Roy Short, Walter Morgan, Vernon Hudson, John Connolly, Ken Long and Cyril Davies.

Pupils of Herbert Road School in 1930. They are: back row, left to right: Enid Lewis, May Emmanuel, Dylis Thomas, Betty Cairns, Betty Squires, Netta Herbert, Winnie Phillips, Irene O'Neil, Hazel Thomas, Betty Thomas, Ivy Bryant, Joan Hughes. Middle row: Archie John, Tommy Britton, Peggy Dennis, Glenys Havard, Doreen Becker, Vivienne Hiskins, Neville Cann, Myra Williams, Enid Hendy, Vera Edwards, Evelyn Williams, (First name unknown) Webb, Dennis Jones. Front row: Ronnie Gallander, Freddie (surname unknown), Leslie Jeffreys, Clement Pedlar, Terry Davies, Emlyn Gorman, Harold Hudson, Frank Perkins, Raymond Webb, Ralph Baber, Lemmie Jones, Haydn Howells, Tommy Britton. The teacher was Miss Evelyn Walters.

Standard 1, Melin Girls School 1930. Pictured are: Dora Bromham, Phyllis Jenkins, Rita Douse, Betty Dennis, Iris Williams, Rosy Thomas, Betty Williams, Phyllis Williams, Megan Jones, Val Kingdom, Jean Sim, Beatrice Bryde, Vera Bond, Alma Jennings, Morfydd William, Eileen Daniels, Phyllis Leon, Stella Smith, Marjorie Kinnek, unknown, Betty Talbot, unknown, Nancy Kingdom, Phyllis Chambers, Lilian Bond, Margaret Thomas, Winnie Ball, Dilys Thomas, Edna Morris, Ruby Phillips, Shirley Lodwick, Betty Thomas, Beatrice Mainwaring, Nita Jarrett, Malvenna Harris, Dilys Morgan, Iris Lewis, unknown, Lilian Matherick, Doris Johns, Violet Cox and Daisy Jenkins.

Standard 3, Melin Girls School, 1930 Some of the girls are Mair George, Martha Griffiths, Alma Penny, Doris Matherick, Ada Thomas, Phyllis Howells, Nancy Brown, Dorothy Melin and Greta Williams.

These 10 Melin Primary School girls passed the scholarship to Neath Girls Grammar School in 1947 – a result never before achieved. Back Row: Sheila Watts of Bowen Street; Maureen Jones of Pendrill Street; Lorna James, of New Henry Street; Rita Harrison of New Henry Street and Jean Lake of Old Road.

Front Row: Linda Green of Whittington Street; Valerie Richards of New Henry Street; Valerie Knight of Old Road; Ann Rees of Old Road and Norma Thomas of Bowen Street.

A class at Melin Boys School, in the early 1950s. Back Row, from left: George Allen, Brian Douse, Malcolm Edwards, David Thomas and John Last. Middle Row: Headmaster Mr. Gwyn Alan Jenkins, Brian Gunter, Brian Williams, Albert Baker, David Lewis, Eddie Tucker, Ronnie Williams, Paul Budge, Ronald Jarrett and the teacher Mr. Harris. Front Row: Jimmy Morgan, Larry Davies, Harold Thomas, Terry Heskins, Terry McNeil, John Hill, Peter Davies, Hugh Stacey, Ronnie Breach and Brian Mogford.

These boys from the Melin School are seen at Ogmore Camp in 1952. Back Row: Herbie Jenkins, Joe Farmer, Mr South, Mal Edwards, Ray Scanlon. Front Row: Brian Douse, Alan Jenkins, Vince Scanlon, Ray Jeffs, Brian Williams and Brian Mogford.

This photograph was taken in 1950 in the Melin School. The young boy is Joey Farmer of Crythan Road, who was the head prefect at that time. The occasion was a presentation to the school of a framed photograph of the Mayor of Neath, Councillor Len Burton, on the right, who was a former pupil at the school. Next to Joey is the head teacher Mr. Jenkins.

Coco the Clown visited the Melin Infants School in 1957. The tallest boy in the light pullover is Michael McDonald of Crythan Road. Coco gave out certificates to the children who correctly answered questions on road safety.

A class at Melin Boys' Junior School, 1954. Back row: Jacky Rees, Gomer Richards, unknown, Ronald Gammon, Gerald Budge, Jeffrey Thomas, Roy Morris, Alan Hutchings and Norman Douse. Middle: Roy Phillips, Lyn Herbert, Clive Harris, unknown, Michael Jones, unknown, David Rees unknown, and Alan Brooks. Front: Aubrey Harris, unknown, Ken Jutsam, Tyrone Elias, Gwyn Williams, Derek Blackmore, Eric Rees, John Demery, Peter Morris, David Davies, Mr. Harris, headmaster and teacher, Mr. Davies.

Melin Infants School pupils all dressed up in 1951. Some of those children are: Sian Davies, Susan Clark, Wendy Davies, David Vigors, Michael Richardson, Brian Llewellyn, Paul Clifford, Norman Whomes, Colin Webber, Michael Phillips, Paul Nicholas, Philip James, Robert Kent, Jimmy Davies, Stuart Boyle, Donald Thomas, Kenneth Parr, Bernard Morgan, Gerald Isaacs, Peter Williams, Michael Parfitt, Glenys James, Frank Rees and Michael Gorman.

These 11 young ladies were the Melin School Scholarship girls of 1958. They are: Marianne Russell, Jennifer Ripley, Margaret Vickers, Ann Smart, Christine Price, Gloria Nesbitt, Mary Smith, Carol Jones, Susan Williams, Wendy Rayson and Pauline John.

A Melin School class of 1960 with their teacher Miss John in the school yard. In the background is the Co-op Bakery. Today the site is occupied by a housing complex. Among the class, 12 are scholarship girls and can be seen in their Grammar School Blazers and five are Central School girls. The girls are: Judith Gregory, Joan Griffiths, Christina Clark, Eileen Downman, Cheryl Hargest, Linda Cook, Linda Harris, Kathleen Pickering, Linda Tamplin, Ceri Roberts, Gillian Harris, Ann Jones, Christine Curtis, Helen Magnus, Patricia Lewis, Valerie Evans, Christina Lewis, Susan Lewis, Beryl Hancock, the youngest girl from Melin School to pass the scholarship to Neath Grammar School; Sheila Brock, Peggy Dipple, Pat Davies, Gaynor Rosina John, Gaynor Patricia John, Ann Richards, Jacqueline Warwick, Rosemary Arnold, Carole Williams and Pamela Harris.

Pupils of Melin Infants School, 1961, including: Julie Jachimiak, Penny Griffiths, Hilary Gardener, Jeanette Thomas, Suzanne Jones, Gareth Richards, Christine Sojka, Catherine Lewis, Steven Hemlock, Norma Hinder, Karen Morgan, June Mellin, Christine Wholmes, Maureen Evans, Michael Mills, Robert Mogford, John Ford, Colin Smalldon, Noel Harris, Julie Hughes, Christine O'Shea, Annette Williams, Linda Dunford, Peter Price, Noel Davies, Steven Dyer, Margaret John, John Richards, Clive Jones, Robert Gardner, Linda Holmes and Irene Evans.

These young girls, pictured in the Melin School yard in 1963 all passed the 11 plus and were headed for Neath Grammar School. They are, back row, left to right: Sharon Bailey, Gillian Thomas, Caroline Harries and Eleanor Hardy. Front: Barbara Hancock, Judith Lovering and Caroline Hale.

This photograph was taken at Melin School one St David's Day in the early 1960s. Some of the children dressed up for the occasion are: Ann James, Peter James, Jill Howells, June Powell, Martin Powell, Wendy Flynn, Corinne Lewis, Beverley Reed, David Emanuel, Hadyn Rees, Beverley Jenkins, Nicholas Jones, Sharon Cook, Jeanette Cook, Leslie Packington, Christine Williams, Steve Cook, Kim Hetherington, Christopher Abbot, Lloyd Watkins, Wynford Gillard, Peter John, Deborah Hanford and Paul Davies.

A Melin School Class in 1962/63, with their teacher Miss Morgan. They are: Paul Gregory, Alan Brunger, Robert Buono, Clive Mitchell, R Jenkins, Desmond Cole, John Sparey, Philip Cronin, Hugh Ryall, Vanessa Bond, Jayne Mayers, Suzanne Stone, Corinne Lewis, Elwyn Floyd, Peter Hill, Jayne Ryall, Jill Burgess, Diane Trenberth, Gillian Best, Edward Attard, Lindsay Hambley, Tina Rosser and Terry John.

These boys and girls pictured in the Melin School yard in 1964, are the pupils selected for the Central School. They are: Catherine Lewis, Linda Dunford, Maureen Evans, Isobel Hurn, Christine O'Shea, Jeanette Thomas, Sharman Davies, Christina Sojka, Susan Isles, Karen Morgan, June Mellin, Mark David, Gareth Richards and Michael Mills.

Mrs McCarthy's Melin School class, 1967: Wayne Davies, Michael John, Kevin Williams, Mark James, Peter Lilley, Mark Brettle, Cathy Hanford, Mandy Clarke, Paula Williams, Karen Thomas, Julie Mellin, Teresa Beynon, Teryl Mead and Caroline Shepperd.

The logo on banner behind these pupils, PSS, stands for Pencaerau Secondary School and this photograph was taken there in the early 1960s. The smartly dressed boys include: Alan Brock, Gerald Floyd, Brian Thomas, Clive Thomas, Peter Davies, Wayne Griffiths, Michael Griffiths, Billy Heggie, Terry Probert, Gwyn Davies, Michael Hulance, Clive Tandy, Stuart Morgan, Billy Davies, Robert Jones, Colin Denton, John Holmes, Raymond Nicholas, Martin Shone, Tommy Webber, Brian Clifford, Michael Bannister, Jeffrey James, Alan Nichols, Martin Derrick, Maldwyn Case, Ralph Hutchings, Keith Mills, Carl Gunter and Barry Roblin.

The class of 1968/69 at Melin Junior School. Pictured with teacher, Mr. G.Powell are: Michael Price, Michael Murray, Brian Daniels, Paul Davies, Nigel Morgan, Tyrone Phillips, Gaynor Evans, Angela Mort, Rhia Salmon, Maria Glover, Annette Price, Peter Jeffs, Paul Jenkins, Noel Mellor, Barry Oakes, Catherine Mellin, Sian Edwards, Jennifer Jones, Ann James, Tina Lewis, Donna Reed, Cathy Sperry, Deborah Hanford, Peter Williams, Steven Baldwin, Jill Phillips, Kim Davies, Elizabeth John, Catherine Davies, Robert Davies and Paul Darvell.

Melin Infants School pupils in 1969. Some of those pictured are: Andrew Wosencroft, Kevin Florence, Mark Headon, Neville Mort, Clive Williams, Richard Waring, Paul Hotchkiss, Paul Headon, Linda Beynon, Cheryl Lewis, Heather Allen, Lynne George, Sandra George, Mair Thomas, Carol John, Caroline Stone, Jackie Knight, Sharron Jones, Jennifer Jones, Steve Nicolls, Lance Evans, Andrew Trick, Paul Ferguson, Jeffrey Heskins, Jonathan Pearn and Kevin Collins.

Mrs Morris' class at Melin School, 1968: David Rees, Derek Price, Colin Mills, Wayne Smith, David Bond, Andrew Hayward, Leighton Baker, Russell Arnold, Deborah Sperry, Cheryl Crow, Andrew Gormon, Justin Davies, Denzil Tristram, Wayne Brettle, Paul Thomas, Robert Williams, Robert Gregory, Peter Derrick, Wayne Jenkins, Alison Sparkes, Delyth Jenkins, Karen Jones and Paul Clark.

A Christmas party at Melin School in the early 1970s. Enjoying themselves are: Gareth McCarthy, Neil Davies, Lyndon Matthews, Michael Mainwaring, Neil Mogford, Carl Storey, David Murnane, Jackie Tomlinson, Julie Williams, Jacqueline Reynolds, Diane Harris, Moira Flynn, Jackie Pascoe, Donna Nicholson, Janet Watkins, Ceri Morris, Joanne Hughes, Angela Jeffs, Lorraine Crow, Jackie Witts and Karen Thomas.

Melin School pupils at another Christmas party in the early 1970s. Dressed up in their paper party hats are: Beverley Rees, John Hill, Jonathan Griffiths, Neil Hotchkiss, Richard Weller, Chris Weller, Gary Packington, Annessa Williams, Susan Williams, Allison Matthews, Ann Davies, Denise Ash, Helen Lewis, Susan Waring, Susan Flynn and Heather Morris.

This photograph will bring back many memories for former Melin school pupils. It was taken in July 1967 on the retirement of Miss James, who is pictured outside the school with staff colleagues. They are, back row, from left Mrs Couch, Miss R Jones, Mr G Hopkins, Mr R G Jones, Mr Thornburg, Miss Hughes, and Mrs L Williams. Front: Miss G John, Mr Harries, Miss BV James and Mr Davies.

This photograph was taken in 1967 outside the Melin School, when the Mayor of Neath, Mary Moule presented a silver trowel to the school. It's a beautiful thing in a lovely leather box, and the inscription reads: Presented to Rev T W George, Chairman of Llantwit Lower School Board, upon the laying of the foundation stone of the Melin School, Herbert Road, May 25, 1898. The trowel remains in the school today.

This is the Melin School Football Team of 1964-65, proudly pictured with headmaster Mr Henry Harris and teacher Mr Gwyn Jones, after winning the Neath and District League Tournament. The successful team was: Noel Davies, Brian Lee Captain; Mark David, William Bryan, Douglas Hardie, Clive Davies, Stephen Dyer, Robert Mogford, Gareth Llewellyn, David Short, Rowland Harris, John Richards, Stephen Hemlock and Gareth Rees.

This was the Melin School soccer team in the1972/73 season. Pictured are: back row, from left: Gary Powell, teacher; W Tamplin, M Edwards, J Wilkins, vice captain; V Jenkins, R Arnold, D Spagna, G Winstanly. Front: D Rees, S Morris, L Baker, captain; S Sharp, A Hayward, I Protheroe and K Williams.

The Melin Boys School under-11s football team, 1953. They were the proud winners of the Neath and District Shield that season. They are: back, from left: Mr H Gwyn, headmaster; Brian Mogford, David Joseph, David Thomas, Albert Baker, Alan Jenkins, George Allen, Eddie Tucker, Mr Brown, sports master. Middle: Vince Scanlon, Ronnie Williams, Mal Edwards, captain; Peter Davies, Graham Jones. Front: John Davies and Terry McNeil.

Pencaerau School rugby team in 1954. Pictured are: back, from left: Roy Bish, teacher; Terry Hooper, Keith Jones, Graham Thomas, Royston Lewis and Nye Richards. Middle: David Richards, Martin Howells, Wildrew Clark, Glen Ball, Terry Lowry, Malcolm Walters, Rowland Parker, Mr Williams, headmaster. Front: David Clark, Vernon Thomas, Gareth Davies, David Thomas, captain; David Joseph, Alun Mellin and Peter Davis.

Chapter 4

Shining stars

Many people have set out in life from the Melin and achieved great things in a wide variety of fields. These range from the world of entertainment to top-flight dog breeding. You could say they have helped to put the district on the map.

Among them was Oscar-winning film star Ray Milland who was born Alfred Reginald Trustcott Jones in Exchange Road in 1907, only a few yards from the plaque on the Community Centre which marks the fact. He spent a great deal of his childhood in the Hillside area and attended the Gnoll School and Kings College, Cardiff. At the age of 19 he joined the Royal Household Cavalry where he became an expert shot and a member of the Company's Rifle team, winning many competitions. He served for three years in the Household Cavalry before entering films in 1929. He left for America in 1930 and joined Paramount Pictures. He played many leading roles in Hollywood. In 1945 he received an academy award for his performance in the Lost Weekend.

Oscar-winning Ray Milland signs an autograph for a miner on one of his visits to South Wales.

Oscar-winning actor Ray Milland makes one local autograph hunter happy in the early 1970s during a visit to Gnoll Primary School, Neath, which he attended as a youngster.

This plaque honouring famous film star from the Melin, Ray Milland, was unveiled at Melincrythan Community Centre in 1996.

Maudie's words launched long running TV soap

Maudie Edwards was born in Florence Street on October 16, 1906. Her mother was from Penydre, but grew up in the Melin.

Maudie made her first appearance on stage aged four with her six year old sister May. Their father Ned who was himself a semi-professional entertainer called his two daughters the Two Little Queenies and they performed in workingmen's halls and theatres all over South Wales.

When Maudie was just seven her father died, but she and May continued to work the music halls of Great Britain. On May's tragic death at the age of 21, Maudie continued her career alone. During the war she featured in BBC Radio's Workers Playtime and travelled abroad to entertain the troops.

In the 1940s Maudie topped the bill in many radio programmes and appeared in films such as Pink String and Sealing Wax and Only Two Can Play with Peter Sellers. Maudie was known as a dialectician as well as a stand up comedienne but she also had a good singing voice, providing the vocals for actresses Diana Dors,

Maudie Edwards at the height of her career, and below, being met by her family at Neath railway station on her return from Australia. Maudie's mother Nan is on her left, husband Ralph Zeiler is on her right and next to him her sister Val.

Maudie Edwards and her sister May as the Two Queenies on stage with their father.

Maudie Edwards in full flight during a performance at the Grand Theatre as Aladdin.

Margaret Lockwood and Gene Tierney in various films and she shared the bill at the London Palladium with Frank Sinatra. On December 9, 1960 at 7.00pm Maudie Edwards, playing retiring shopkeeper Elsie Lappin, spoke the first lines on what was to become the world's longest running series, Coronation Street. But Maudie had other talents too. On January 26, 1953 the Palace

Maudie Edwards in typical vivacious pose.

Theatre, High Street, Swansea became home to the Maudie Edwards Repertory Company. On the opening night on January 26, 1953 patrons queued around the theatre in pouring rain until it was officially opened by Councillor W T Mainwairing-Hughes.

That night, Dear Evelyn was the play on offer and it received a great reception. Maudie had the power to draw guest actors including Glyn Houston and Philip Griffith to her theatre. Even that however, was not enough to secure her survival and her link with the Palace came to an end during December 1955.

In 1950 she had supported Frank Sinatra at the London Palladium for two weeks. On her weekly radio programmes she had her own theme song introduction where the announcer would croon:

"I bring you the voice of the people, from over the hills and dales, and the voice of the people is brought to you, by a voice that comes from Wales."

Maudie died in London on March 24 1991, aged 85.

William Squires

William Squires was one of Britain's most talented actors. A star of stage, screen, radio and also TV, he was born in Florence Street on April 29 1916 and attended the Gnoll and Cwrt Sart Central schools. In his youth he was employed at the Eaglesbush Tinplate Works. He left Neath in 1933 to seek employment in London, began to take an interest in the theatre and won a scholarship for two years study at RADA. That was the start of a distinguished acting career which included an appearance at the Old Vic in a Shakespearean role during 1946.

He played character roles in many films, such as Dunkirk, The Man Who Never Was and Alexander the Great. In 1956 he was in the epic film, The Battle of the River Plate, the true account of the sea battle in 1939 between the German battleship Graf Spee and the British vessels Ajax, Achillies and Exeter.

In 1961, he began a two-year Broadway run when he took over from Richard Burton in the stage version of Camelot, playing King Arthur with co-star Julie Andrews. In 1969 he was Thomas Moore in Anne of a Thousand Days and in 1978 he was Gandalf in the animated version of Lord of the Rings. One role that he will be remembered for is that of chief spy hunter in Callan, William died in 1989, aged 73.

GAIL PEARSON

Gail Pearson was born in Walters Road. The daughter of County Councillor Mel Pearson and his wife, Sheila. She attended the Melin School, Cwrt Sart Comprehensive and Neath College. Gail went on to take a Bachelor of Music degree at Cardiff University. From here she went on to the Royal Northern School of Music for two years gaining two more diplomas. She is acknowledged as having a wonderful musical talent like that of her father Mel Pearson, one of Neath's most celebrated musicians.

In 1992 she made her Glyndebourne debut singing Jana in Janacek's Jenufa. She had sung in the Glyndebourne chorus for the two previous years. Gail has covered many roles with the Welsh National Opera Company and countless others with both the English National Opera and Scottish Opera companies. She also took a role in an opera with Placido Domingo in the Bastille in Paris. Gail is still a freelance opera singer.

Emlyn — he's tops in Welsh Terriers

Emlyn Snow outside Felstead Kennels in the Eaglesbush Valley.

Emlyn Snow's father Harold started breeding dogs in 1923, under the affix Brynmelyn, the name of his house in Danygraig Road. In 1928 he was granted the Felstead breeding affix and Welsh Terriers were introduced to the kennel (Felstead was the name of the Derby winner that year). Although Harold died on New Year's Eve, 1979, Emlyn continued to show and breed Welsh terriers and has maintained the high standard for which the kennel is renowned. He was only six when he began kennel work and when his father entered him in the children's class at a Neath show which took place in the Drill Hall.

Emlyn's first judging appointment was at Alexandra Palace Open Show, London, when he was 20 years old, and he has gone on to judge at many shows since then. Like his father before him, he has judged at Crufts, and keeping up tradition, Lynn Snow, grandson of Harold and nephew of Emlyn has also judged at Crufts. Three generations judging the same breed at the most famous dog show in the world is an enormous achievement.

Felstead Kennels has been breeding and showing Welsh terriers longer than anyone else in the world, and there have been countless UK and overseas champions. With such a record, these kennels are a legend, a wonderful tribute to Emlyn and his father before him and a feather in the cap of the Melin! In 1998 an American woman, Bardi McLennan, published a book entitled The Welsh Terrier Leads The Way. The high esteem of Emlyn and the Felstead fame is apparent throughout the book. She states in it that the Felstead Kennels is no doubt the largest and most venerable Welsh Terrier kennel anywhere in the World. The dogs are kennelled in a beautiful facility in a park-like setting which we know as Eaglesbush Valley.

Emlyn Snow as a young man, showing off a champion Welsh Terrier under the watchful eye of his father Harold.

Chapter 5

Times of toil

Industry in all its many guises has long played a part in the everyday life of the Melin. Many aspects of metalwork provided employment for the area's families at one time or another along with other smaller, but equally important enterprises.

The clock seen in the picture opposite is the old Melin Works clock which today is displayed in the reception area of the Castle Bingo premises. It was salvaged and restored by Castle Leisure and its final resting place is only a matter of yards away from where it was originally sited, high above the Melin.

The clock had been a prominent feature in the area since the old Melin Tinplate Works was opened in 1864 by businessmen Flower and Leach. Mr Flower was an old boy of Winchester School. Its motto was Manners Maketh Man which the Melin School adopted and still ascribes to today.

The works were constructed for the manufacture of tin and terne plates, of which a total quantity of 100,000 boxes (6,000 tons) per annum were produced, employing from 500 to 600 workers and supporting a population of several thousand. In connection with the manufacture of tinplate Messrs Leach, Flower & Co carried on the business of Japanning or decorating by a process patented and introduced from France, of which they had the control in the United Kingdom. These decorated tin plates, produced in every variety, design and colour were mainly exported and also used extensively for tea, match boxes, biscuit boxes and other articles of domestic use.

Regarding the Melin clock, I received a letter from Mr Harry Hughes who lived in Skewen. Harry was an apprentice in the Melin Works in 1936 and part of his Saturday morning duties was to climb a rather rickety stairway in the finishing department to oil and wind the

clock. His wage at that time was 7/6d (37 ½p). Prior to that Harry worked in the Cold Roll department and bundled scrap for 11 shillings (65p) a week. He had a scar on his leg to prove it. A gash on his leg from an unfortunate accident had been stitched and clipped by Dr. Coyne who had a surgery in the Melin.

Although Harry had lived in Skewen for over 40 years, he still regarded himself as a Melin boy. He was born in Southgate Street, one of seven children: Vera, Addie, Emrys, Mervyn, Myra, Billy and of course himself. His sister Myra had worked in the Melin Post Office prior to emigrating to Long Island in the United States in 1947. She was a GI Bride and married an American serviceman after the Second World War.

The clock on the Melin Works viewed from alongside the Cryddan Brook, in the early 20th Century.

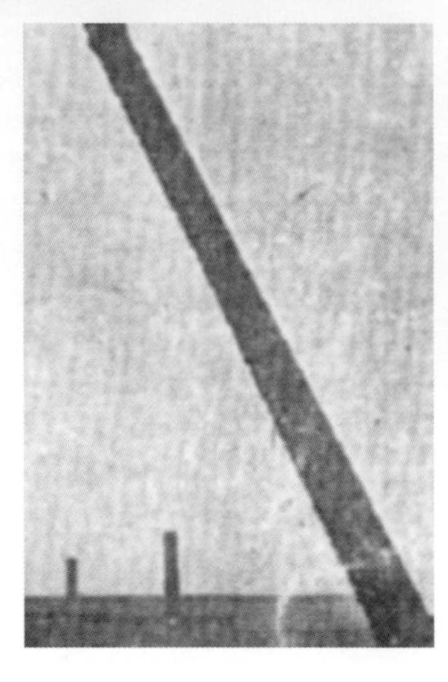

The Melin Tinplate Works stack disappears from the skyline in 1952. Built in 1864, it was 195ft high, making it the tallest in all the works around Neath. It had been a landmark for 88 years. Steeplejacks took four days to demolish it. Bricks from the stack then went into the new building erected on the site by the Baglan Engineering company.

They might look like mere boys, but these lads were in fact employees of the Melin Tinplate Works in 1916. Dorothy Morgan of Lewis Road loaned the photograph and said her father, Will Isaac, is among them, as are his brothers, Albert and Jim. They were from Charles Street. Two other brothers are also pictured, Bert and Ivor Knight. One other name known is Harold Dennis.

Workers at the Melin Tinhouse, around 1927/28. Christine Phillips from Bryncoch loaned the photograph. Her grandfather, Sidney Wall, is sitting at the front far left. He was from Cecil Street and appears to be about 15 or 16 at the time it was taken..

This photograph was taken to celebrate the opening of the Eaglesbush Factory in June 1935. On it can be seen company officials and local councillors. Among those present were Sir Robert Barlow, of London, Mr Cunliffe, manager; Tom Davies, John R Williams, Edgar Davies, office manager; Bill Thomas, works engineer; Bill Jones, Ivor Thomas, union rep; Mr Peterson, an American; Marsden Jenkins, draughtsman; Tom Falcon chief tinplate inspector; Morton Smith, Councillor Tom Cole, Frank Smith, Bill Dennis, George Hopkins, chief cashier; Ivor Dunford, Billy Miles, David Rosser, in charge of the mills; Ossie Lloyd, in charge of wages; George Hieder, director and John from Penywern.

This wonderful photograph shows workers in the Galv in the 1930s. It belongs to Harold Gully, formally from George Street, and he is among those pictured. They all look quite contented, I wonder if it was the beginning or end of their shift. Notice some of them with their lunch boxes and billy cans. It seems in those days most of the young men wore flat caps. Mr Gully can't remember much about it or any of the names. One thing he does remember is cutting sheets for the air raid shelters during the War.

Melin tinplate workers in the late 1920s. Leyshon Lewis, from Howells Street is second from the right.

Leyshon Lewis busy at work on a Roller Mill in later years.

Workers at Eaglesbush Works in 1920. This picture from the past belonged to Cyril Edwards of George Street. The men all wore flannel shirts to soak up the sweat and carried towels around their necks for the frequent job of drying themselves off.

Two of Cyril's brothers are in the photo, Ernie Edwards, a furnaceman and Edgar Edwards who was what was referred to as a behinder. Edgar died at an early age. Among those hard working men pictured left are Carlo Harris, Bertie Broad, Jonnie Rees and Tom Dennis.

These men are from the number three and four mills at the Melin Galv Works. They are celebrating the Coronation of George VI on May 12, 1937. Among them are: Billy Williams, Amos Cooksey, foreman; Frank Brenton, George Dobbs, Danny Long, Mr Richards, Ernie Cousins, Reg Elias, Gilmor Williams, Bertie Ware, Frank Richards, Frank Hooper, foreman; Tom Gossedge, Johnny Davies, George Penny, Dick Lester, Joe Harrison, Frank Jeffs, Dick Charles, Roy Cousins, Sam Rees, Will Rogers, Joe Glover, Dai Evans, Tudor Moule, Will Thomas, Alf Moxley, Ernie Payne, millwright; Dick Mogford, Mr Jenkins, Ben Dennis, Arthur Williams, Sam Davies, Arthur Williams, Will Davies, Charlie Humphreys, Chimo, Glyn Lloyd and Fred Monkton.

The Neath Steel Sheet and Galvanising Company's Air Raid Precautions Staff in September 1939. Back row, from left: A Thomas, A Hopkins, S Wagstaff, A Moxley, S Mogford, J Harrison, R Rees, HL Griffiths, HR Parnell and G Hancock. Third row: E Matthews, P Davies, E Walter, DJ Evans, TS Gossedge, W Meredith, E Mill, AE Davies and F Cooper. Second row: TJ Thomas, D Roberts, H Hanford, G Rosser, S Gill, WC Hawkins, J Bennison, I Burrows, WT Giddings and C Trick. Front row: Ald WK Owen, R Monkton, JB Ashton (LAGC), HP Lloyd, managing director, Mrs HP Lloyd, JS Mill, Morgan Morgan and Bert Sutcliffe.

This was the Eaglesbush Works Band in the late 1930s. There are a number of Neath Mayors among them including Emlyn Emmanuel, Len Burton, Alderman Jack Morgan, Alderman Lodwig and DC Griffiths. His name will always be synonymous with the Melin owing to the fact that a road was named after him, DC Griffiths Way which was formally Chemical Works Road. Others in the picture are Sidney Jones, works Manager; George Haider, director; Edgar Davies, office Manager; John Penywen Davies, coldmill superintendent; David Rosser, mills engineer; Sid Davies, chairman of Neath Rugby Club and formally from Bush Row; Nathaniel Davies who had a fish and chip shop near the former Co-op store in the Melin; Walter Jenkins, Fred Roberts, Arthur Roberts, Marshall Roberts, Billy Roberts, Billy Miles, Alec Monkton, George Vickery, Alfie Stinchcombe, Reggie Jones, Mr Gammon and bandsman Vernon Ellis from Helen's Road. Sadly not long after this photograph was taken Vernon died in the war, it was only 10 weeks after joining the Navy that his ship HMS Frazer was sunk in action.

Volunteer helpers at Payne Street Soup Kitchen in 1926, the year of the General Strike, the long miners' lock out and widespread unemployment. Some of those pictured are: Councillor Katie Davies, Mrs D Richards, Miss Hopkins, Mrs Nel Flaherty, Miss Blodwen Williams, Mrs George Griffiths, Mrs Taylor and the solitary man, Mr Tom Thomas.

The smart uniformed men were all drivers and conductors of the former Richmond Bus company seen in the early 1940s. The company's offices were on the top of Osborne Street. In the 1950s the United Welsh Company took over the running of the Richmond operation. Mr Williams, the owner, can be seen in the centre with his son next to him, the only two not in uniform. Among those in the picture are Terrence Roach, Kenneth Roach, Ernie Webb and George Williams.

Locomotive men from Neath Locomotive Sheds at Penrhiwtyn. They are seen with their spoils after a successful performance in the British Rail Knockout Darts Cup Final, held at the Cambrian Inn, in the Melin in 1958. Those top darters are, Back row, from left: Reg Chapman, Ron Evans, Jack Johns, Danny Jones, and Gerald Pavey. Front: Terry Howells, Danny Davies, Peter Davies, Terry Profit and Mal Isaac.

Pictured in the mid 1950s is the manager of Provident Personal Credit Limited, Reg Semmens, with agents, on their way to canvas in Cimla. Mrs Thelma Tomlins, far left, retired after 34 years with Provident. Three other of those agents are Muriel Jeremiah, Elsie Nettle and Anne Hughes.

Engineering staff of the United Welsh Bus Company in 1955. Included are Bob Merrick, Doug Thomas, David Clarke, Ossie Davies, Freddie (surname unknown) and Bill Hopkins.

Some of the employees of the Metal Spinning factory at a function in The Highbury Country Club, around 1969. Among them are Mrs Anne Williams of Westbourne Road who worked for many years in the canteen; Mrs Griffiths, Katy Evans and Margaret Ballinger. Katy and Margaret were supervisors. During the War Margaret and her husband Billy Ballinger kept the Farmers Arms Pub in the Melin. The women are pictured with Jock, a line supervisor.

Some of the DS Smith staff who attended the company's annual dance at the Empire Ballroom in 1958. Among them are Eileen Callaghan, David Knight, John Gittins, Anita Cosker, Myra Swaffield, Pearl Walters, Margaret Thomas, Esme Joseph, supervisor; Violet Edwards, Bella Mizen, supervisor, whose parents kept the corner shop before Loverings, John Jones, Ronnie Breach together with Vic Downs and his wife.

Members of the despatch department of the Midland Metal Spinning Factory in the early 1960s. The factory closed in 1975. Among them are: Maralyn Rosser, Dorothy Snow, Beryl Madge, Molly Gorman, Katy Roberts, Morwena Jenks, Edna Morgan, Irene Thorne, Margaret Glynn, Ray Davies, Betty Weeks, Ceridwen Osborne, Margo Spencer, Mrs Carter, Shirley Carter, Gertie Carter, Del Lloyd, Irene Sparkes, Jackie Turner, Peggy Shewry, Bron Jenkins, Ray Holloway, Janet Tamplin, Lynne Watkins, Rosemary Harris, Margaret Morgans, Muriel Whitelock, Joan Williams, Mair Gill, Christine Davies, Doreen Rosser, Carol Leah, Olive Lewis, Norma Breach, Cherry Bater, Christine Anthony, Carol Phillips, Joyce Howard and Linda Davies.

A gathering of former employees of the Neath Steel Sheet and Galvanising Company shortly before the closure of the works in 1982. Among them are: John Glover, Ron Treharne, Sidney Wall, Jack Pike, Ron Parnell, Gwyn Parnell, Viv Griffiths, Dai Roberts, Glan Morgan, Ted Deere, Spencer Stevens, Tom Beaton, David Twining, Doug Meredith, Peter Brennan, Trevor Evans and Managers Peter Latham and Ivor Gwyn Davies.

Workers at the DS Smith carton factory take a break from their labours. They are John Evans, Dennis Wathan, David Knight and Ron Penhalligan.

Management and office staff of the Metal Box Factory during a function at the Castle Hotel, about 1960. Front row, from left: Sybil (surname unknown), Betty Davies, Mary Parker, Carol Barnett, Phyllis James, Joan Bromham, Orville John, Ann George, Betty Parker and Gladys Hughes. Second row: Tom Knight, Irene Bowen, Davies Bennett, Gwyneth Dyer, Bill Doughty, Alex Hamilton, Blod Bater, Roger Gray, Luther Davies and Harold Hayward. Third row: Denvil Pickerell, Lil Williams, Sadie Lloyd, Mary Jeavons, Lyn Davies, Norma Rees, Barbara Smith, Marslie Harris, Russell James, Edna Richards, Randall Williams, Ann Moody and Bill Edmunds. Back Row: John Martin, Len Davies, Len Dawes, Glan Davies, Sheila Prosser, Mary Llewellyn, Joan Evans, Gerald Lawrence, Mary Davies, Noel Mort, Beryl Davies, George Brophy, June Simms, Myra Davies, Mary James, Beryl Glendenning, (Unknown), Madeline King, Val Thomas, Ann Thomas, (Unknown), Barbara Keen, Ray Gwynne and Carolyn Egan.

These men were attending a Metal Box Cricket Club dance which was held at the Beach Hotel, Port Talbot, sometime in the 1960s. Back row, from left are: Raymond Carr, Billy Thomas, Jack Anthony, Vernon Hooper, (Unknown), Alan Jenkins, David Williams, Roy Jones, Norman Whitelock and Sam Jones. Front: Malcolm Rogers, Mr Brophy, personnel manager and Len Jordan.

Canned Food Week meant a tasty trip to the Metal Box factory!

In a Melin School essay book from the 1950s one of the contributions is entitled The School Visit to the Metal Box Factory. It was written by pupil Sheila Evans.

The essay tells all about how some of the Melin schoolgirls visited the factory during Canned Food Week in June, 1959. On arriving at the factory, they were given a talk on the plant's production process and the company's machines.

The Metal Box, wrote Sheila in those distant days, employed 2,000 people at that time and made 100 million ends and tops for cans per week. The pupils walked in and out of the machines and saw the railway which had been built inside the factory to transport the items manufactured.

She said she found the lacquering machine the most interesting. The lacquer was applied by rollers and hardened in long stoving ovens.

Later the girls went upstairs and sampled some of the tinned food that eventually ended up in the cans the Metal Box produced. 'That was delicious,' she wrote. Then it was a short walk back to school to end the trip.

When Sheila wrote her essay, the Metal Box had been one of Neath's main employers since its opening in 1936. At that time there were just 30 women employed there, by the early 1950s that number had increased to 1,700 women, and the number of full-time employees later rose to more than 2,500.

Who are these happy people enjoying themselves at a grand party? Well the time is 1937, shortly before the Second World War. The venue is the Metal Box factory canteen and the event is a Christmas Party. As the Metal Box factory was built in 1936, this was probably the first childrens' Christmas Party to be held there. A few of those smiling faces belong to Ruby Harris, Lyndon Lewis, Maisie Thomas, Gladys Weeks, Olive Davies, Nancy Hill, Don Collins, Violet Williams, Bertie Mellin, Ivor Davies, Fred Tucker, Lillian Thomas and Ivor David.

Canteen assistants at the Metal Box factory during a visit by Her Majesty Queen Elizabeth II during 1977 which was her Jubilee year. Among those pictured are: Lillian Lye, Jean Veale, Beatrice Griffin, Nancy Davies, Margaret Slee, Connie Stokes, Margaret Newton, Nancy Dale, Sylvia Richards, Margaret Bowring, Gaynor Thomas and Kitty Penny. The man with glasses in the foreground is George Hunkin.

The management team at the Metal Box factory in August 1979. They are: Back row, from left: Ian Martin, Meyrick Sheen, Dudley Thomas, Peter Smith, Eric Alderson, Emlyn Williams, Noel Mort, David Emery, Roy Cherrett, Donald Jenkins, Neville Lewis, Paul Strong, Richard Parsons, Ray Britton, Walter Barnes, Frank Prout, Ronald Price, Bob Bird, Gareth Jones, front; William Anderson, distribution manager; Keith Barnes factory accountant; John Wildman, general manager; Tony Pegg, senior personnel manager and Gareth Thomas, technical manager.

Pictured outside the Melin Works, is a memorial stone for employees who fell in the Great War 1914 - 1918. It was discovered when the works was being demolished in 1994. Melin businessman Cliff Lovering spotted it in a pile of rubble and conveyed it in a trolley to the corner shop in Exchange Road which was then run by his son Robert. It was later cleaned and, thanks to Neath Town Council, a permanent home was found for it at Melincrythan Community Centre. Here is a roll call of the 23 men whose names appear on the stone: Thomas Anthony, WJ Bevan, Walter Bishop, John T Brooks, Bertie Broome, Jeffrey Clifford, Hubert S Davies, John Edwards, Ivor Griffiths, William Hooper, Hopkin Hopkins, Alcwyn Jefford, Harry Jenkins, Edward Jones, William Jones, Thomas Lewis, William Lewis, Charles Morris, David Phillips, Albert Rees, John Rees, Harry Thomas and Willie Williams. Most of these men were part of Kitcheners first army of 100,000 volunteers and died in action, including the Battle of the Somme. On that fateful day in 1916 the British casualty toll was 54,470 with 19,240 killed. This battle was the most costly in terms of loss of life, in the history of the British Army.

Neath Town Council

A Service to Mark the Re-Dedication
of a Memorial Stone
in Tribute to Men of the
Melin Works Who Lost
Their Lives in
The First World War

At

Melyncrythan Community Hall

on

Friday 23rd June 1995 at 7:00 pm

The cover of the programme produced for the ceremony held to mark the re-dedication of the memorial stone commissioned to commemorate those employees of the Melin Tinplate works who were killed in the First World War.

Placing wreaths at the memorial stone to the men of the Melin Works who died in the First World War and which is now sited at Melincrythan Community Centre are Town Mayor, Brian Warlow and President of Neath Royal British Legion branch and Councillor Malcolm Gunter. Also pictured are councillor Mary Gunter, Rhydian Smith and Rector of Neath, Canon Stephen Ryan.

Peter Smith with his sons Gareth, aged nine and Rhydian, aged five, at the memorial stone which bears the name of his great uncle Bertie Broome who died during the First World War. Bertie served in the 8th Battalion Welch Regiment and was killed in Gallipoli, aged 26. He made it on to the beach, but was shot by a sniper on Sunday August 8, 1915. Bertie Broome's name is also on the Helles Memorial in Turkey. There is no grave but his panel number is 140. Bertie was one of five children born to Jennie and Rhys Broome, who kept the King William IV Public House in the Green. It wasn't only Bertie who worked in the Melin Tinplate Works, but also his sisters Nellie and Martha.

Neath Town Mayor, councillor Derek Vaughan pays tribute at the Melin Works memorial at Melyncrythan community centre, in 1995, along with councillor Malcolm Gunter, president of Neath Royal British Legion; Viv John, branch chairman NRBL and councillors Walter Noonan and Albert O'Callaghan along with the Town Mayor's Chaplain, Rev Gareth Thomas.

Mervyn Davies of Briton Ferry formally from Ethel Street is a member of a group called Friends of the Lapwing. In 1945, after taking part in the D-Day Landings, HMS Lapwing was one of many ships that took part in the Russian Convoys. Two miles off Murmansk, German U-boats sank the Lapwing, 153 men perished and just 48 survived. A relative of Mervyn's, able seaman Robert Stark from Cornwall was among those who died. Another was able seaman Raymond E Palmer from the Melin. Mervyn was trying to find out, through my column, if there were any relatives still living locally. Thanks to a call from Martin Palmer in Skewen, it was revealed that there were. He related that able seaman Raymond Palmer was his uncle. His father Cyril James Palmer was Raymond's brother. The Palmer family lived at White Rose Villa, Pencaerau, Old Road. Raymond it seems had been an apprentice butcher. He was only 18 when he perished on the Lapwing.

His sister Eileen Palmer fought to have his name put on the cenotaph at the Gnoll Gates where it is now visible for all to see along with all the other brave men who gave their lives in both world wars.

Every year David Flynn faithfully attends the Remembrance Day services in Neath and the Melin, proudly wearing his father, Fred Flynn's medals. For more than 50 years Fred had never missed a Remembrance Parade and David is honoured to continue in his footsteps. Fred Flynn served in the Royal Welsh Fusiliers and it was just at the end of the war that he was wounded. In fact it was on St David's Day, March 1, 1945. He was too ill to receive his military medal in person, but it was sent to him from Buckingham Palace in May 1945. It was 51 years later through the determination of the members of RAOB that Fred was finally presented with his campaign medals. He died in 1996, aged 78. His bravery and courage will always be remembered.

Christmas gift Glen's family had dreaded

Glenville George Williams lived in Bryn Road, Hillside, where his mother, Elizabeth was the proprietor of a corner shop. The business was subsequently run by her daughter, the late Ivy Thomas.

Glenville was educated at Alderman Davies' School and a local private commercial school. He left for London in his early 20s to take up a position with Selfridges the famous departmental store.

At the age of 28 the world and his career seemed to be opening up for him when he was promoted and transferred to the firm's subsidiary, Whiteway's in Penang, Malaya. In 1940 he enlisted, as did most male civilians there, in the Malay Defence Force, a type of regiment like the Home Guard. He was taken prisoner at the fall of Singapore and was sent to the infamous Burma – Siam railway building project. Nothing was heard of him until January 1943 when his mother received a Red Cross card from the prisoner of war camp where he was being held.

As his sole close surviving relative, his niece Cynthia Rees of Cimla, recalls that the first news of his death came in May 1945 as the street party to celebrate VE Day was about to begin in Bryn Road. At just six years old she did not really understand what was happening. What she remembers though are the tears and the grief of the adults at the time. Confirmation of his death did not come until only four days before Christmas on December 21, 1945. He had died of malnutrition in Quiee Camp, Thailand on October 22, 1943 aged 23. Although documents record him as a member of the Malay Defence Force, the Colonial Office considered him a civilian prisoner.

Glenville George Williams

What an amazing abundance of medals is being displayed by these men, all employees of the Great Western Railway at Neath. Some had served in the First and Second World Wars. Among those identified are Bert Anderson, Harry Merchant, Sam Morgan, Eric Edwards, Bill Hughes, a locomotive driver and Harold Gardiner, a signalman.

Chapter 6

May Day magic

May Day in Melyncrythan was the brainchild of Charles Henrywood who in 1982 called a meeting of all voluntary organisations in the Melin area to help plan a charity-based community event for the May Day Holiday.

Its purpose was to provide family friendly entertainment in the locality while helping local organisations raise funds and at the same time strengthen community spirit.

The meeting whole-heartedly supported the idea and in 1983, the first May Day Festival was held. The chairman was Charles Henrywood, Secretary Rita Williams, and the Treasurer Raymond Hale. There were no less than 18 organisations present resulting in a great success with £600 raised for Neath General Hospital at Penrhiwtyn.

This was only the beginning and as the years passed, many thousands of pounds were raised for various charities. Since that 1983 May Day, officers and committee members changed a number of times. All however, have played their part in helping the success of the festival. Glan Mogford took over as chairman in 1994, and Edith Gallanders followed until 2000, while vice chairman was Viv O'Shea. There have been a number of secretaries, including Christine Longman, David Lewis, Nancy Evans and Ron Gallanders and treasurers duties have been carried out by Ken Longman, Ashok Patel and Ron Gallanders.

The year 2000 was the last May Day in Melin, but after a break of five years it was resurrected thanks to the ever faithful Charles Henrywood.

Maypole dancers at Evans Road playing fields.

The first May Day presentation evening in 1983 when £600 was presented to a representative from Neath General Hospital. Also in the picture are Councillor Charles Henrywood, chairman; Rita Williams, secretary; Raymond Hale, treasurer and councillor and Mrs Bill Cotton.

Maypole dancers who took part in the May Day in Melin event, 1994.

Maypole dancers from Melin Junior School, dancing in Neath town centre.

Heading up Crythan Road are dozens of runners who took part in the May Day in Melin Fun Run, 1992.

Winners of the May Day in Melin, 1992 Fun Run with Neath's Town Mayor, councillor Sheila Penry and Mayoress Mrs Nancy Evans.

Members of Siloh Chapel were ready with cakes for hungry visitors in 1993.

Really enjoying themselves at their stall, are these members of the Womens' section of Melyncrythan Choir.

President of May Day in Melyncrythan, Charles Henrywood presents a shield to Jeffrey Evans, the captain of the winning team in the event's Inter-club pub quiz 1996. Looking on are team members Alistair Dacey, Jan Dacey, Byron Rogers and Margaret Rogers.

This model created by 90 year old John Thomas of Brookdale Street, was the centre of attention at the May Day exhibition held at Melin Infants School. John's scale model of a steam engine was just one of many marvellous hand-crafted items on display.

Winners of a painting competition held as part of the May Day in Melyncrythan celebrations in 1992. They are Daniel James, Nicole Wales, Gemma Vaughan, Thomas Bartlett, Gemma Jones, Jamie Roberts, Naomi Davies, Rhys James and Clare Rees.

Neath Mayor, Councillor Charles Henrywood and Mayoress Mrs Josie Henrywood pictured in 1995 with officers and committee of the May Day in Melyncrythan event.

The 1995 May Queen, Louise Evans, and her attendants; Ceri Holmes, Karen Smith, Stephanie Cross, Danielle Watkins, Nadine Thompson, Kendal Evans, Lauren Phillips and Joanna Heard.

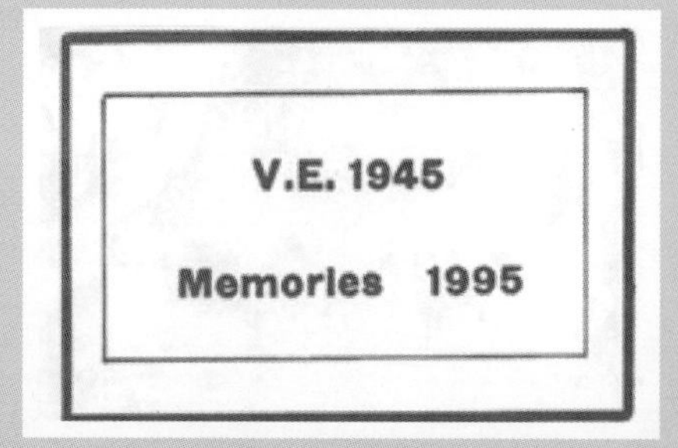
V.E. 1945

Memories 1995

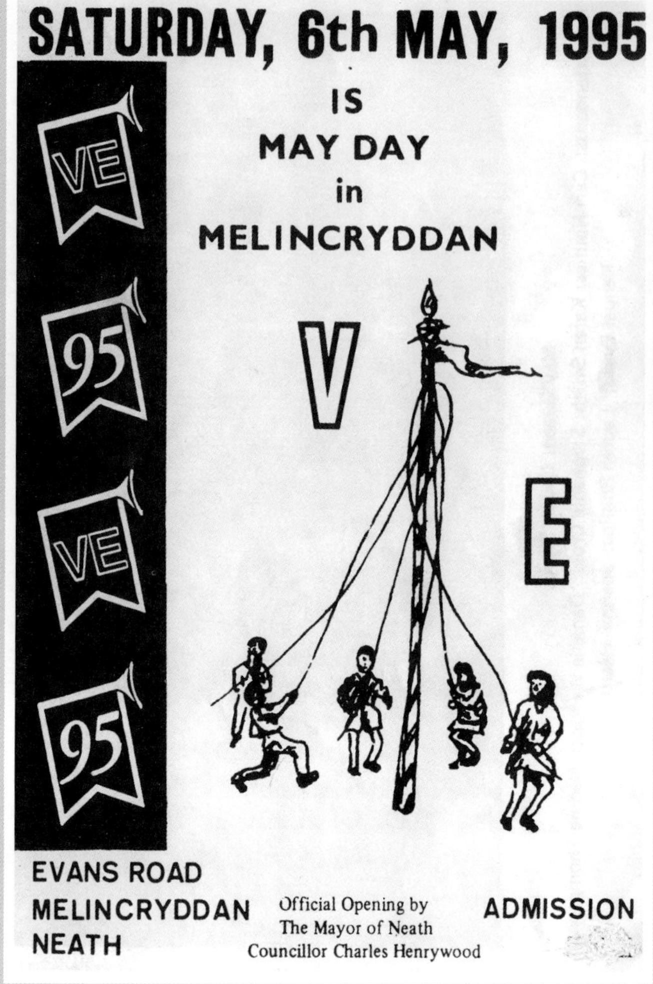

The cover of the special programme compiled to mark the 50th Anniversary of VE Day in 1995.

After nearly six long years of loss and destruction the war in Europe came to an end on May 8, 1945 - VE Day. Fifty years later in 1995 some residents shared their memories in a special May Day programme.

Mrs Betty Rees, Bush Row
She recalls the street party in Briton Ferry while her late husband Percy was in East Africa. He was a coxswain with the Air Sea Rescue service.

Mr Jack Thomas, formerly Mary Street
He was in Luneburg, Germany where the Germans offered their surrender to Field Marshall Montgomery.

Mrs Sylvia Taylor of Mile End
She was in Neath Hospital awaiting the arrival of her baby. Lorraine was born on May 11.

Mrs Nell Harris, of Southgate Street
Every window in the street had a jam jar with a lit candle in it as there was no more black out.

Mrs Sarah Dummer, of Furnace House
She remembers the Street party with beautiful pastries made with liquid paraffin.

Mr Gerald Jenkins, formerly of The Mount
Gerald was in the Civil Defence and often manned the telephone in the gasworks to sound the air raid siren for Neath.

Mrs Phyllis Lloyd, of London Road
She lived in Jersey and remembers how exciting it was to pull down the white surrender flags and fly the Union Jack.

Mr Gordon Jenkins, of Bowen Street
He was in Rookwood Hospital, Cardiff with his war injuries on VE Day.

Mr Ron Sterry, of Whittington Street
Ron served in the Royal Marine Commando and was in Etienne in Holland where crowds of excited people and brass bands filled the streets.

Mrs Gladys Thomas, of Brookdale Street
She still has the coveted stainless steel dish she won in her street party.

Mr Frank Storey of Burrows Road
He was in the cinema in Resolven when a message that read: the war is over was flashed on the screen. Everyone rushed out into the street and began dancing.

Mrs Doris John, of Florence Street
Doris was at work in the Royal Ordnance Factory in Bridgend while on that day her husband Lew, an RAF pilot, was released from a Prisoner of War camp.

Mrs Cherry Brown, Furnace Terrace newsagents
Crowds made their way to Neath town centre, some to the Cambrian Hotel, but there was no beer there.

Mrs Audrey Jenkins, of Old Road
How marvellous it was to hear the church bells ring after six years of silence. If a church bell rang, it could previously have been warning of an invasion.

Mrs Alma Boyle, of School Road
Alma served in the Land Army. On VE Day she was visiting her father in Neath Hospital. He had been injured in an accident at Thos. Ward's while her husband Jock, wounded in Germany, was in hospital in Newport.

Mrs Esther May Williams, of Furnace House
She recalls the street party. Her home had been bomb damaged.

Mrs Phyllis Roderick, formerly of Crythan Road
Their party was held in Neath Boys Club.

Deputy Mayor of Neath, councillor David Davies and Deputy Mayoress, Mrs Barbara Davies at the crowning ceremony of Janine Pugh as Melyncrythan May Queen, 1992. With Janine is her chief attendant Lianne Lewis and attendants Louise Clarke, Carly James, Danielle Cole, Lindsey Allen, Leanne James, Rachel Howells and Natalie Williams.

May Queen 1994, Zoe Cook with her chief attendant Stevey Leigh Radford and attendants, Cala Waites, Danielle Parkes, Anna Hale, Lesley-Ann Peck, Louise Firth, Jennifer Francis and Natalie Clarke.

May Queen, Sadie Marie Gillard, presents a cheque for £1,000 to sisters Yvonne Evans and Karen Grant of the Childrens Ward at Neath General Hospital. The money was raised from the May Day Festival in 1993. Also in the picture are May Day president, councillor Charles Henrywood; chairman, Glan Mogford; vice chairman, Viv O'Shea; secretary Ron Gallanders; treasurer, Ashok Patel and committee representatives.

Queens of

The 1997 May Queen Ria Olinski and her attendants, Laura Davies, Helen Morgan, Jennie Holmes, Samantha Lewis, Stacey Arnold, Kelly Hopkins, Jessica Davies and inset, Kathryn Barwick.

May Queen in 2000 Kerry Anne Morgan with attendants Angharad Jones, Kirsty Murphy, Lyndsey Jones, Jennifer Norris, Hannah Mathews, Samantha John, Sophie Jayne Jones, Kirsty Harris and Catherine Salter.

Three good community causes benefited from the 1999 May Day Festival Fund. Melin Junior and Infants Schools and Neath General Hospital's breast clinic received cheques from May Queen, Danielle Morris and Borough Mayor, Malcolm Harris at a special ceremony held at the town's Royal British Legion Club. Also pictured are Melin Junior School head , Julie Whitehouse; Infants School deputy head teacher, Eunice Walters, vice chairman of the May Day Fund, Rita Williams; Dr Chris Flowers from the breast clinic; Town Mayor, Doreen Davies, May Day Fund president, councillor Charles Henrywood, fund chairman, Edith Gallanders and secretary Ron Gallanders.

May Day

May Queen in 1998, Stephanie Slaughter, and attendants Kylie Lake, Jodannah Jones, Emma Jones, Laura Williams, Lauren Dunn, Aimee Gilbert, Alesha Jones, and, inset, Kate Edwards.

May Queen and attendants 1996. They are: Ashley Barnes, Masura Begum, Natasha Rowlands, Kayley White, Nicola Richards, Eloise Collier, Alys Firth and Bethan Roberts.

A total of £500 was raised at the May Day in Melyncrythan Festival 1995, for the breast services ward at Neath General Hospital. Handing over the cheque to staff nurse Beverley Killa is Neath Borough Council Leader, Charles Henrywood.

Town Mayor, councillor Albert O'Callaghan handing over a cheque to Melin Infants head teacher, Miriam Powles. The money was raised from the May Day Festival in 1998.

May Day in Melin 2000, helped raise hundreds of pounds for charity, including cancer sufferers from Neath and Port Talbot. A cheque for £1,000 was presented to Y Rhosyn, a day centre at Neath Hospital which helps cancer sufferers. Pictured at the presentation, from the left are Neath Town Mayor, Alun Cooper; Mayoress, Tina Cooper; May Queen, Kerry Morgan; Lynne Sheridan of Y Rhosyn, Neath Port Talbot Deputy Mayoress, Doreen Davies and Deputy Mayor Des Davies.

Chapter 7

Happy times

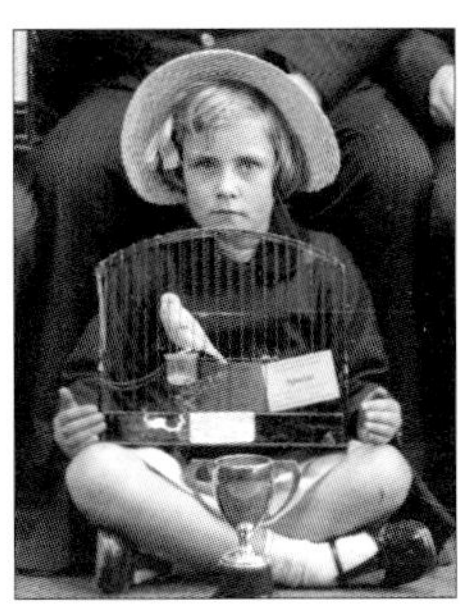

Like all other communities, there is a time for work, rest and play. Down the years the community of Melincrythan has relaxed and enjoyed itself in all manner of ways with parties and parades plus exciting excursions all playing a part.

These are times when the community unites in a desire to forget the troubles and woes of the world and just be happy and have fun. Just like this band of people below, photographed in 1937, celebrating the Coronation of King George VI at a party in Howells Street, now Dan-Y-Graig Road. Some of those partygoers are Audrey Snow, Maureen Williams, Jean Elias, Freda Thomas, Violet Jones, May Thomas, Cyril Prior, Vernon Dummer, Muriel Joseph, Danny Evans, Mr Bowen, Freda Chambers, Ken Steer, Megan James, Lucy Slee and Mrs Jenkins (Jinks). She ran a shop in her front room and two items she always had on sale were Spanish root and syrup of figs.

Four local women in a mock-up studio car used by photographer, Harry Jones of Windsor Road, Neath, in early 20th century.

Union jacks, bunting, party hats and cakes. These five ladies had them all! They are pictured in Howells Street in 1953, celebrating the Coronation of Queen Elizabeth II and are, from the left: Violet Jones, Lorna Harris, Meirwen Parry, Freda Chambers and Eileen Hetherington.

Four bathing belles near the dock bridge on the Neath canal alongside the Metal Box factory in 1937. Miss Mainwaring, Bessie Jones, Thelma Lawrence and Nelli Cann were all from Grove Lane and had been swimming in the canal.

This photograph was taken in the late 1940s during Neath Carnival. Mrs Audrey McDonald of Crythan Road, can be seen standing on the extreme right. Some of the other clowns, mostly from the Penrhiwtyn Street area are: Louie Hendra, Cynthia Penny, Mary Jones, Ivy Charles, Gloria Pitman, Joyce Chambers, Will Smith, Phyllis Smith and Irene Jenkins.

Residents of Burrows Road at a street party to celebrate the Coronation of Queen Elizabeth II in 1953. Among them are Sylvia Storey, Gillian Walker, Muriel Walker, Maggie Mayers, Betty Williams, Lynne Williams, Katie Jones, Peter Heatherwick, Roger Andrews, Julie Holwill, Ken Holwill, Beattie Hancock, Linda Richards, Glenys Williams, Keith Williams, Brian Heatherwick, Vera Noonan, Gladys Lewis, Edith Gallanders, Phyllis Pugh, Netta Hughes, Ivy Mayers, Gwennie Richards, Florrie Evans, Annie Evans, Mary Hughes, Mrs Walters and Mrs Edwards.

Among these children in fancy dress are Alun Mellin, Hywel Green, Vivian Lake, Sheila Davies, Pamela Davies, George Sly, Michael Richards, Clive Lake, Mair Parry, Jeffrey Evans and Joyce Lake. They had gathered for the Evans Road celebration of the Coronation of Queen Elizabeth II, in June, 1953.

Residents dressed in Victorian costume sometime in the 1980s outside Stockham's bakery. Among them are Mr and Mrs Dimaio from the No 1 Cafe; Mr Fisher the chemist; Val Snow, Pam Arnold of Top Pets; Edna from Stockham's; Tina Linciano the hairdresser, Suzanne Davies, Mary Burford, Pauline Anthony. Adrian from Denade is seated proudly in the centre as Queen Victoria.

On their first holiday after the war, which was to Blackpool in 1948, these four women who all worked in the Japan Works went to see famous singer Joseph Locke in a show and were thrilled to meet the famous singer after the show and pose with him for a picture. They are, from left: Brenda Gibby, Brenda Hurcombe, Val Prothero, and Marion Brocksopp.

These happy gentlemen were enjoying a Boxing Day party in the Butchers Arms, 1958.

They are, at the back, from left: Malcolm Wiltshire, Haydn Hughes, Darryl Lennon and Raymond Langam. Front: Dennis Wiltshire, Eric Becker, Bryn Davies and Bernard O'Keefe.

At a presentation in 1991, local members of Neath Royal British Legion, pay tribute to their longest serving committee member, Sid Rees, centre, who was retiring after 37 years. President Meyric Thomas was also honoured with a special certificate for his service. Five members, Glan Pascoe, David Huckridge, Gerald Williams, Mike O'Connor and Raymond Hale were appointed vice presidents during the evening.

Neath and District Charity Darts League presented cheques for £100 to Bryncoch and District branch of Athritis Care and £100 to the orthopaedic department of Neath General Hospital. Pictured, from left are: Dennis Curtis, league secretary; John Griffiths, card secretary; Joan Nash of the Bryncoch branch; Malcolm Isaac, chairman; Councillor Raymond Williams, Borough mayor; Raymond Thomas, chairman of Ynysygerwn Cricket Club; Reg Semmens, treasurer of the darts league; Mayoress, Rita Williams and Mike Davies, orthopaedic surgeon at Neath Hospital.

Colin and Dewi, landlords of the Cambrian Arms, present a cheque for £535 to Lynne Sheridan, nurse in charge at Y Rhosyn, Neath Port Talbot Hospital.

Members of Melincrythan Amateur Operatic Society in 1937 when they performed the Student Prince. The two principal singers were Idris Morgan and his wife Violet who went on to sing with the Carl Rosa Opera Company. They were both members of Siloh Church. Their daughter is the well known BBC Wales broadcaster Anita Morgan.

The Melincrythan Amateur Operatic Society's first production was in 1923, called the Dogs of Devon.

In May 2003 they celebrated by presenting 80 Years of Song at the Gwyn Hall. Here's a poem written about our own operatic society

One of the best

The MAOS are one of the best, as music societies go
Since their very beginning, they've always been winning, the hearts of the audience aglow
It was in a coal yard they had their first start rehearsing for their very first show
Called then the Danygraig Choral Society, not MAOS as we all know
The show was Dogs of Devon, I believe, and the date 1923, I perceive
So 80 years on those years that have gone, have always spectacular been
With the players a class of their own, giving all whether big part or small, 'till that final curtain fall
Many now have gone but the show always goes on with talented youngsters on hand
Whether singing or dancing or simply back staging, they're all just one happy band
So to celebrate those wonderful 80 years, it's the Gwyn Hall once again for those cheers
In this month of May. And enjoy their 80 years of song.

Members of the staff at Metal Box and Eaglesbush, who took part in the successful production of Carousel, by Briton Ferry Amateur Operatic Society in 1972. Pictured are Linda Mort, Tudor Allnut, George Sylvester, Wayne Kenure, David Sylvester, Brian Headon, Neil Howells, Elaine Parker and Lynda Evans.

Engine trouble forced the aircraft of pilot, captain George Pond, left and Cesare Sabelli, right of councillor Joe Brown, Mayor of Aberavon, to make a forced landing on Aberavon Beach on Thursday May 24, 1934. When the Mayor visited the scene of the emergency landing he was accompanied by Superintendent Rees Davies, of Glamorgan Constabulary and Miss C Deeble, town clerk's secretary. Mrs May James, from New Henry Street provided some interesting information about the photograph. She said that when Prime Minister Ramsey Macdonald visited the area, which was on numerous occasions, Joe was his right hand man. At one time Joe and his wife, Jane, kept the Somerset Arms in Taibach. Their son George Brown was the Manager of the South Wales Transport bus company's garage in Eastland Road.

Neighbours from Albert Road enjoying a game of cricket in 1953. They are, from left, back row; Ernie Brock, Haydn Best, Rex Crew and Vernon Emmanuel. Front: Will Emmanuel, Stephen Mainwaring and Viv Mainwaring. If this photograph was taken today, in the background would be Morgan's Road flats as Albert Road was demolished around 1966. Betty Eckett's father and brother are pictured, they both worked in the Eaglesbush factory. One memory she had of Albert Road is a party they laid on for Ernie Brock when he returned home after being a prisoner during the Second World War.

Daytrippers prepare to set off from outside the Grandison Hotel is sometime between 1905 and 1915. The tall man standing in front of the pillar was landlord of the Grandison, William Stevenson.

Members of the Neath Cage Bird Society with their cups and winning birds after a successful show on January 28, 1939.
They are, back row, from left: L Branch, F Wainwright, H Knight, H Dyer, F Hope and T Hopkins. Front row: D Hughes, T James, secretary; E Payne, chairman; E Thomas, assistant secretary and E Speed. The young girl in the front is Miss Thomas. After the picture appeared in my column, I received a phone call from Terry Hughes in Cilfrew who had a sad story to tell about the photograph. His father Darrell Hughes is in the picture. He was only 16 at the time and can be seen proudly holding a cage containing his winning budgerigar. Darrell was from Pendrill Street and when German bombs fell on Pendrill Street, one hit Darrell's aviary and killed all his birds. Another story I was told by a reader was that at the time she worked for Peter Moruzzi who owned the Cosy Cafe in Windsor Road. She recalled when these bombs dropped on Pendrill Street. The shock killed a pet canary which was in the kitchen of the cafe. Mr Moruzzi was remembered as the most wonderful man. He was one of 700 Italians on board the Arandora Star bound for Canada when it was torpedoed on July 7, 1940, about 125 miles north west of Ireland. A total of 486 Italians were lost at sea that day. This disaster also affected other Italian families in Neath including the Cavallis, the Minettis, The Solaris and the Spagnas.

Annie Harris, outside her house in Bowen Street during celebrations to mark the Silver Jubilee of King George V and Queen Mary in 1935. For many years Annie was a white coat in the Metal Box. With her are Garfield Johns, Jimmy, Tommy and Freddie Cork, Freddie Roberts and Harry Jenkins.

Chorus members of Melyncrythan Amateur Operatic Society's production of Oklahoma at the Gwyn Hall in 1956. They are Beryl Hardwicke, Beryl Rouse, Audrey Jenkins, Barbara Jones, Carol Gray, Betty Orum, Pat Tustin, Thelma Edwards, Lynne Huckridge and Jill Bird.

Neath businessman George Mayers with his wife Matilda and children, Olive, Beattie, Dorothy, Arthur, George, Brynmor and Tillie. They are at the rear of their fruit and veg shop in Briton Ferry Road in the early 1920s.

Officers and committee of the Neath branch of Athritis Care at their headquarters, the Pensioners' Hall in Wellfield in the 1980s. Among them are five founder members: Alan Michael, Olga Freeman, Dorothy Morgan, Lillian Phillips and Jocelyn Larke. Cyril Niven, also a founder member, was not present as he was in hospital at the time. With the Mayor, councillor Iris Hobbs is branch president Graham Hale and his wife. Others pictured are KC Martin, Pat Martin, Sylvia Michael, Viney Rees, Jean Jones, Russell Workman and Tony Mathews.

A presentation event at Neath Royal British Legion Club in 1971. The recipient is the woman seated in the front, Miss Thomas, who was a tireless charity worker. Alongside her are treasurer George Hopkins and chairman Jack Brocksopp. Standing at the back, from the left, are vice-chairman, Margaret Gamlin, Eileen Cooksey, Arthur Gamlin, Marion Brocksopp, Chris Gay, Betty Rees, Louise Thomas, Teddy Rees, Edie Bevan, May Thomas, Iris Slocombe and Dil James.

Remembering bygone days are the youngsters of New Maria Congregational Church, during celebrations to mark the 50th Anniversary of VE Day in 1995.

They were days many would want to forget. Days of wartime rationing, air raids, great loss of loved ones.

But even among such sadness, there were still moments which strengthened the spirit and resolve to win through. Many of those moments were the singing of unforgettable songs such as Tipperary, Seigfried Line, Lili Marlene, Blue Birds over the White Cliffs of Dover and many others from both world wars that were sung by children and adults alike. Many at the celebration event were dressed as they would have been in the 1940s. There was also an exhibition of wartime memorabilia, including gas masks, tin hats, ration books, and actual newspapers of those war years.

Before the entertainment, a wartime meal of corned beef, mashed potatoes and peas, followed by rice pudding, was enjoyed by the 65 people who attended.

Proceeds from donations and the evening's entertainment were given to Ty Hafan Children's Hospice. This amounted to £400.

Melyncryddan Gardening Society pumpkin competition winners Megan Slocombe, Nathan Jones, Victoria Soames, Lewis Richards, Nathan Williams, Matthew Elliot and Chloe Soames.

These boys were swimming in Neath canal near the Galv and the gasworks in 1943. They are David Newton, Emyrs Newton, Graham Price, Philip Smith, Tommy Harris, Gordon Soper, Raymond Fellows, Roy Parker, Jackie Pascoe, Donald Wileo and Dennis Edwards.

Canal capers

Youngsters enjoying themselves in the water of Neath Canal near the Melin Works during the 1930s. All from Melin School, they are Raymond Hale, David Davies, Margaret Newton, Glyn Rees and Francis Clifford.

Residents of the Helen's Road area prepare to celebrate the Festival of Britain, 1951. They are outside Herbert Road School, now Melin Infants.The Festival Queen was Madeline Beynon who is in the front row in a long dress. Others include Pat Tomlins, her attendant, Alf Herbert, Arthur Jones, Sid Heskins, Dai Howells, Thelma Bridgeman, Martin Bridgeman, Alan Mogford, Roy Heskins, Lilly Tomlins, Thelma Tomlins, Ralph Jones, David Jones, Gerald Harris, Wendy Rosser, June Lovering, Olwyn Floyd, Olga John and Mayor of Neath, Gil Rosser.

Children of N & C Luxury Coaches staff at their Christmas party, 1951.

Landlord and landlady of the Cambrian Arms, Mr & Mrs John Griffiths, presenting a colour TV for use in Ward 3 in Neath General Hospital and £86 for its Children's Ward. Pictured from left are John Griffiths, Sister Julie Watkins, Staff Nurse Peter Davies, Nurse Jean Chick and Ann Griffiths, along with regulars of the Cambrian Arms.

Pat Taylor, with John Holding, landlord of the Royal Exchange, present cheques to a representative of the renal unit at a Cardiff hospital. The other woman in the picture is Ceri Davies. It was in 1985 that Pat underwent a kidney transplant and it was in the years that followed she helped raise much needed funds for this worthy cause. Pat, from Briton Ferry Road, was one of the Melin's much loved characters with a warm and friendly disposition. She worked for many years as a lunchtime supervisor at the Melin Junior School and was highly regarded by all the children and staff. She was the longest serving dinner lady in the school. She was great to have around.

Members of the 5th Neath Guides and Brownies at their HQ in Neath on Tuesday, September 17, 1991, when Ruth Henrywood of Meadow Road was presented with her Baden Powell Trefoil Badge by the Mayor of Neath councillor Ray Williams. Also pictured are Mayoress Rita Williams; District Commissioner, Lesley Matthews; 5th Neath Guiders Elaine Aveline and Caroline Ellis, Brown Owl Judith Clarke and Tawney Owl Christine Longman.

NEATH GIRL GUIDES ASSOCIATION

President : Mrs. E. E. Gibbins

OPENING OF
Guide Headquarters

on

MONDAY, JUNE 1st, 1964

by

OLAVE LADY BADEN-POWELL, G.B.E.
WORLD CHIEF GUIDE.

The cover of the official programme for the opening of Neath Girl Guide Headquarters in 1964.

At the Melin Junior School in 1992, three members of the 5th Neath Guides were presented with their Baden Powell Certificates, the highest award in Guiding. They were Rachel John and Kelly Chambers, both aged 15 and from Pantyrheol and 14 year old Joanna Gibbons of Meadow Road. Either side of the Guides are Leaders Elaine Aveline and Caroline Ellis.

Residents of Florence Street, dressed up for Neath Carnival in 1951. Carrie Davies is in the policeman's outfit. Also there are May Spreadborough, Rosie Ern, Gladys Griffiths, Stella Bentley and Laura Perry, with her young daughter, Jennifer.

Residents of Whittington Street at a VE Day party in 1945. Some of those enjoying themselves are Glaslyn Griffiths, Emily Woolacott and daughter Kay, Avril Griffiths, Janice Webb, Annie Healey, Florrie Anthony, Eric Stillman, an evacuee from London; Marilyn Rees, aged 5 at the time, and seen with her mother Mary Staines and grandmother Julia Staines; Hilda Spares with her baby daughter Barbara. The other baby in the photo is Terry Whitelock. He's in the arms of his grandmother Rose May Knight and near her is Terry's Mother Alice Maud Whitelock.

Some of the residents of Florence Street enjoying themselves at their Festival of Britain Tea in 1951. Pictured with Bruno the dog are May Spreadborough, Rosa Jones, Gladys Griffiths, Stella Bentley and Mrs Laura Potts. The six year old dressed as a cowboy is John Southard

A group of Melin women at a Pensioners Tea at the Wellfield Hall in the late 1950s. They are Margaret Mayers, Mrs Hancock, Mrs Evans and Mrs Harris all from Burrows Road; Mrs Mort and Mrs Brooks from Exchange Road; Mrs Lil Williams from Payne Street; Mrs Mary Jane Harding from Elias Street and Jane Tamplin and Jen Williams from Crythan Road. Another pictured is Maggie Thomas of Marshfield Road whose granddaughter Ann, who she brought up, went on to marry the television personality Michael Aspel.

Pictured in Blackpool are David Watkins (Tusky), who, with his wife Margaret kept the Prince of Wales pub in the Melin for a number of years. Also pictured are Vernon Thomas, Dai Stokes, Peter Rees, Bryn Vaughan, Terry Gregory, David Coleman, Clive Brooks, Gwyn Norris, Denis Davies, David Pascoe, Alan Hutchins, Martin Wagstaffe, Brian Harrison, David Richards, David Saunders, Lyn Jones, Brian Spreadborough, Ivor Amos, Roy Richards and Raymond Morris.

Members and officials of the Neath branch of the Royal British Legion at the send off party for pensioner members on August 1, 1968.

They toured the Vale of Glamorgan on funds raised by members. Included are Cyril Lewis, branch vice chairman and William Edward Watkins. William was born in 1889. He had worked in the Galv and saw active service in both world wars. When the First World War broke out in 1914, he was 25, and volunteered in the Second World War at the age of 51. He saw action in North Africa and Italy. He was a chairman and committee member for many years at Neath Royal British Legion. He had lived in Ivy Avenue and later at Old Road, Melin, where he died in 1981, aged 92.

Another person in the photo is Glyn Jefford, Glyn lived at Pine Grove in Cimla. At one time he worked at the St Ives Pub in Neath, which was owned by his sister Lillian Mort. He later worked at the Metal Box Company. In the front of the picture is Ivor Thomas, branch secretary since its formation in 1921, when he was member No. 72. In 1968, however, following the deaths of old soldiers he was member No. 1.
Others present include Gwyn Price, Eric Ryder, David Ivor Evans, Alan Smith, Ernie Smart and Lew Hodge. Lew and his wife Violet lived in Alice Street. Lew worked in Llandarcy refinery. During the Second World War, he served in the Royal Engineers and was in the Normandy Landings. He died in 1985, aged 84.

Racing, football and a famous star

These men are pictured outside Neath railway station, in 1954, before setting off on a trip to London. They are members of Neath Catholic Club or Paddy's as it was known. Among those pictured are: Bernard Alan, one time steward at Paddy's; Ron Probert, Will Alan, senior; Willy Alan, his son; Gerry Newams, Dai Burrows, Gerald Watkins, Idris Mathews, Dai Davies, Glyn Morgan, Peter Parsons, Herbert Brooks, Ivor Davies, John Carsley, Will Mogford, Will Francis, Bernard Goodall, Iorwerth Stewart and Val Berni. The trip lasted from Tuesday to Sunday, and during this time they visited Ascot for the races, watched Arsenal at Highbury before finishing up with a visit to the London Palladium, where they saw the entertainer Danny Kaye. What an outing it must have been!

Residents of New Henry Street celebrating the Coronation of Queen Elizabeth II on June 2, 1953. Among them are Agnes Collins, May Edwards, Nelson Edwards, Michael Edwards, Nellie Brinfield, Mary Beynon, Alan Newton, Rita Harrison, Lorna James, Shirley Freeman, Brian Tamplin, Mrs Tranter, Mrs Hughes, Kay Newton, Rita Berni, John Bowen, Malcolm Collins, Richard Bowen, Raymond Bryant, Myra Jones, Elaine Griffiths and Pat Beynon.

This happy band from Danygraig Road is celebrating the Queen's Silver Jubilee in the Melyncrythan Amateur Operatic Hall, 1977. Among them are Helen Moore, Tony Moore, Kitty Mellin, Mr Press, Brenda Wassell, Mona Joseph, Rae Davies, Wendy Davies, Jason Davies, Zoe Adams, Michael Lawrence, Sarah Phillips, Jason Davies, Nicky Thomas, Sheila Davies, Karen Davies, Jason Edwards, Gillian Mathews, Barbara Thomas, Wayne Thomas, Jackie Davies, Rita Williams and her parents Richie and Isobel Petherick.

The staff of the Melin Co-op store in 1921. In the middle row far right is 13 year old Cyril Edwards from George Street. He spent all his working life at the Co-op, starting as a warehouse boy and working his way up to manager of the store's shoe department. In his capacity as manager he travelled all over the country. He even met Sir Stanley Matthews at a shoe and leather fair in Yorkshire in 1953. Other staff members are G Edwards, grocery, D Rosser, butcher, P Williams, provisions; Tom Harris, manager; Miss Duffield, drapery; Miss Vizor, office; V Rosser, warehouse boy and EM Jones, grocery.

At a shoe and leather fair in 1953, football star Stanley Mathews shows a pair of new football boots to Cyril Edwards, the manager of the shoe department at Neath Co-op. The boots were designed by Mathews and Mr Grainge, manager of the Co-op's footwear factory at Heckmondwike, Yorkshire. It was in 1953 that Mathews steered Blackpool to one of the most extraordinary victories in the history of the FA Cup Final. At the time, Britain was in the midst of Coronation euphoria, and the new Queen was to be guest of honour at Wembley. Mathews, a footballing great, was deemed to be past his prime at the age of 38. He had already lost two cup finals and this one would surely be his last. Blackpool went down 1-0 within 2 minutes, but Mathews inspired his team back into the game. Even when 3-1 down he didn't give up. In that last minute of the match he set up a goal that clinched a 4-3 victory. The sporting historians decreed that it should forever be remembered as Mathews' Final.

A party in Old Henry Street, opposite the Borough Arms to celebrate the Silver Jubilee of George V in 1935. The partygoers include George Stanley Walters, his son Arthur, Bramwell Davies, Beattie Lewis, Violet Lewis, Elizabeth Lewis, Phyllis Brice, Betty Evans, Janet Walters and Mrs Knight.

Seen during one of their rehearsals are the Melin Follies with their compere Jimmy Jones. The Follies were a group of ladies from the Melin Social Club who raised a lot of money for charity from their wonderful shows. From left to right in back row are; Veronica Lewis, Joan Cummings, Lorna Lucas, Connie Wozencroft, Jimmy Jones, Glenys Williams. Seated are Patsy Davies, Florrie Jenkins, Dita May, Norma Walsh and, in front, Judith Bryant.

It was all the fun of an open-top charabanc for this outing in 1929. Those enjoying themselves were residents of Florence Street.

This Melin-based accordion band was very popular in the early 1940s. The teacher was Iris Spurry, who is on the top left. Others include Alma Spurry, Lottie Thompson, Hilda Youatt, Violet Probert, Eileen Drew, Iris Nicholas, Barbara Pascoe, her brother Donald Pascoe, John Thomas, Vernon Phillips, Arthur Prothero and Trevor Hillier.

Committee members of Melin Social Club around 1975. At that time Gordon Jenkins was chairman. Others pictured are Peter Parker, Glyn Joseph, Brian Dawes, Ernie Hunt, Ken Moran, Bill Bennett, Bernard Payne, Cyril Pascoe, Harry Collier, Terry Lloyd, Neville Norris, Joe Rees, Tom Morris, Don Morgan, David Wathan and Les Clarke.

Entertaining ways of some popular Melin musicmakers

Making music has always been a popular pastime in the Melin. Whatever the instrument, it seems that someone, somewhere in the community plays it, both young and old alike.

Mrs CC Lewis, who will be better known to many as Lottie Thompson, was one of those and recalled her involvement with the piano accordion and other musical instruments.

"When I was a young girl in the 1940s," she said, "I used to play the piano accordion. My teacher was Iris, the daughter of Nan and John Spurry, who kept a parlour shop in School Road until they moved to 51 Briton Ferry Road, between the premises of William Brettle the butcher and the Cambrian public house. It was there that they opened a haberdashery shop until it closed in the 1970s.

"We paid one shilling a lesson which was sometimes held in Mrs Spurry's kitchen and sometimes in the nearby Neath Boy's Club, next to the Post Office in Briton Ferry Road. We did wartime charity shows for the fire service, played at a Swansea hospital, a sergeant's mess at Jersey Marine and a Metal Box factory concert compared by Graham John who worked there.

"Everyone had to do something other than playing the accordion. Sheila Ballinger step danced; tenor Vernon Phillips from Pencaerau, sang Vienna City of my Dreams and other beautiful songs. Iris played a Gipsy mood music solo , with her long black hair and dressed in a satin blouse, gipsy skirt and bolero, looked the part. In the second half, the boys dressed as cowboys with Scout hats, lambskin chaps and plaid shirts. The girls wore silk blouses, khaki pleated skirts and Scout hats too. We all sang and played cowboy songs. Four of us girls, with Violet Probert playing the drums, played dance music for the soldiers. Sadly Iris died in childbirth in 1949, aged just 22.

"I have so enjoyed playing music ever since and later replaced the piano accordion with an electric organ. I have spent many hours of total enjoyment and

Penrhiwtyn Street residents dressed up for Neath Carnival, early 1950s. Among them are Edith Delve, Cynthia Penny, Mrs Joseph, Mrs Madderick, Joyce Chambers, Audrey Chambers, Ivy Joseph, Mr Hendra, Mr Madderick, Morfwyn Mogford, Mrs Francis, Mrs Butler, Mr Scaplehorn, Mrs R Hendra, Mrs Drummer and Phyllis Delve.

Regulars of the Builders Arms, all in Neath Rugby Club jerseys, before a trip to Ireland to watch an international in 1994. They are Les Thomas, Ceri Stillman jnr, John Sperry, Colin Tomlinson, Craig Brown, Steve Thompson, Keith Widlake, Mal Thomas, Bobby Turner, Andrew Wozencroft, Steve Thomas, Leighton Soper, Ceri Stillman, Arthur Trick, Dean Jones, Paul the landlord and Glenville Davies.

Children from Bowen Street, at the seaside in the early 1950s. Among them are Roy Phillips, Alan Brock, Sheila Brock, Stuart Morgan, Pat Morgan, Elizabeth Brock, Christopher Brock, Gareth Brock, Marlene Brock, Rosalind Williams, Tasmin Brock and Megan Rees.

Rugby mad regulars of the Royal Exchange pub at Cardiff Airport on a trip to Paris in 1981. Among them are landlord John Holding, Chris Johnson, Peter Rees, Gary Jones, Mick Williams, Charlie Cardiff, Haydn Bop, Malcolm Tills, Sykie, Ralph Williams, Chris Abbott, Sackum, Smiler, Terry John, Decca, Tubby Derrick, Billy Lloyd, Lyn the Gas, John Rowlands, Milson Knight, Arthur Trick, John Gosney, Morton Lilley and Dennis Chief.

This picture was taken in the King Edward Hotel in London Road around 1957. Little did one of them, Miss Arm, think that what she had started with her ballet training class in the Pensioners Hall in Wellfield would evolve into Neath Ladies Keep Fit Club which over the years has gone from strength to strength. From the right the women are Doris John, Miss Arm, Mrs Howells, Betty Poley and Betty's sister, the three ladies standing are Valerie Snow, May Rosser and Joan Morgan.

Valerie Snow of Neath Ladies Keep Fit Club between Rita Cole, treasurer and Bette Amphlette, assistant treasurer, at a celebration dinner commemorating the club's 50th year of existence.

Members of Neath Keep Fit Club at their Christmas Party in the RAFA Club, 2009. They are Megan Fraser, Irene Selby, Kaye Anderson, Norma Wilkins, Valerie Snow, Pam Curtis, Rita Charlton, June Baker, Valmai Wiltshire, Valmai Ball, Bette Amphlett, Eirwen Davies, Valerie Parsons, Mary Morris, Alice Gregory, Kath Canfield, Joyce Knight and Janet John.

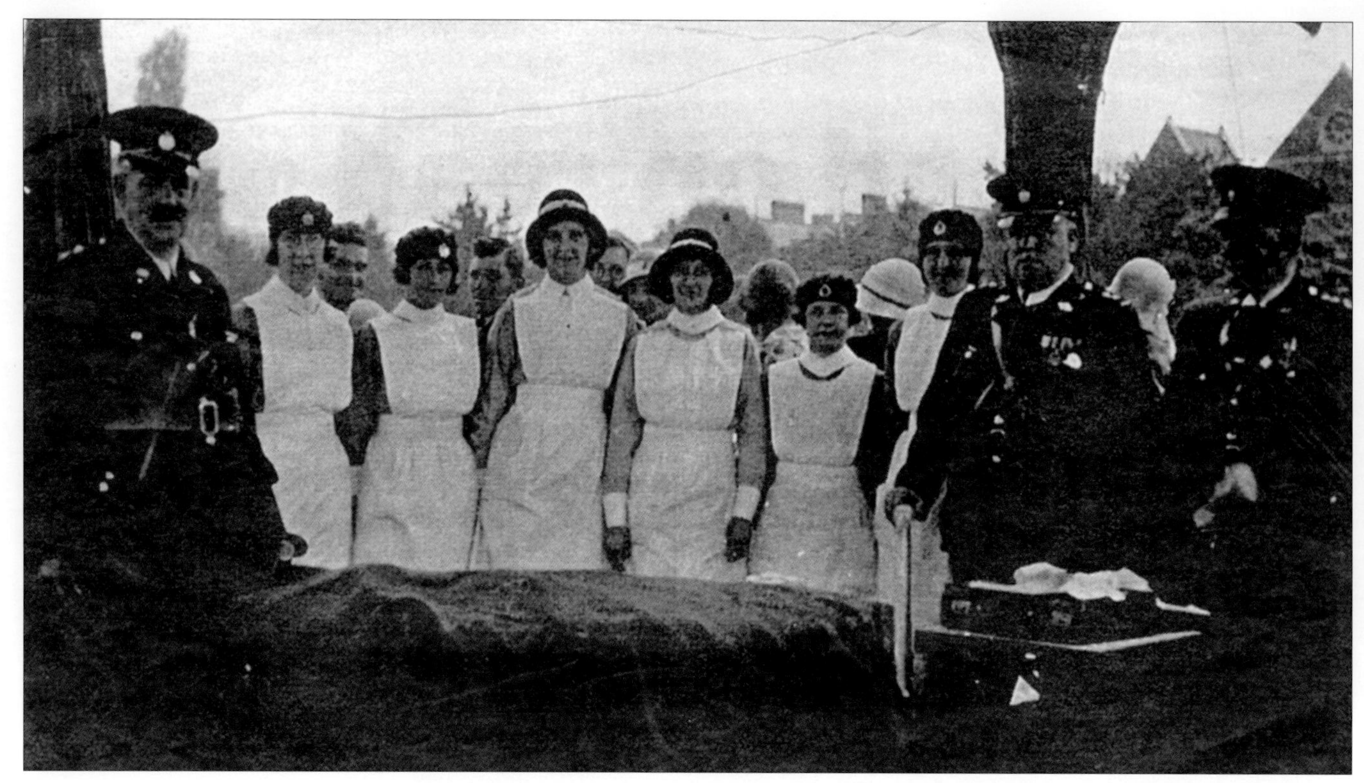

This photograph was taken in the bandstand at Victoria Gardens, Neath in 1934 when the St. John Ambulance Brigade was in attendance for the National Eisteddfod which was held in the town that year. Pictured second on the right is Hugh Benjamin Gardiner. He was the founder member of brigade in Neath and along with two of his sons, Hartley and Ivor, built the St John Ambulance hall which stood in Wellfield for many years. Also included above is Ivy Thomas who had a shop in Bryn Road. She worked hard for Neath Boys Club and Kidney Research. Among the other women are May Williams, Ethel Pearce, Ethel Morgan and Doris Powell.

A party held to celebrate the Investiture of the Prince of Wales at the Farm School, Hillside, in July, 1969, with many residents of Bryn Road, Wallace Road and Coronation Road donning fancy dress for the occasion.

Chapter 8

Worshipful ways

Religion has played an important part in the life of the Melin almost from the time it was just a tiny hamlet. Its people have long gathered in churches and chapels in times of sadness and times of praise.

Among such places of worship is St Catherine's Church. Its foundation stone was laid on the March 21, 1889 by Miss Place of Neath, on a site given by Edward Evans of Eaglesbush House. The completed church was consecrated on Thursday, April 23, 1891 by the Lord Bishop of Llandaff, the Right Reverend Richard Lewis. The buildings architects were Mr DM Davies of Neath and Mr Carter of the firm of Seddon and Carter.

The church was dedicated to St. Catherine in tribute to the late Mrs Catherine Place, who for many years ministered to the needs of the sick and poor and who was also one of the church's principal founders and left a substantial legacy of £500 to the building fund.

The Bishop took the Communion service and the first sermon in the church was delivered by the Rev FW Edmondes. The preacher at the evening service that day was the Rev TW Welby.

And so the church of St Catherine's began its first 100 years of life, built to serve the Melin community at a cost of £3,000 and able to accommodate 500 worshippers.

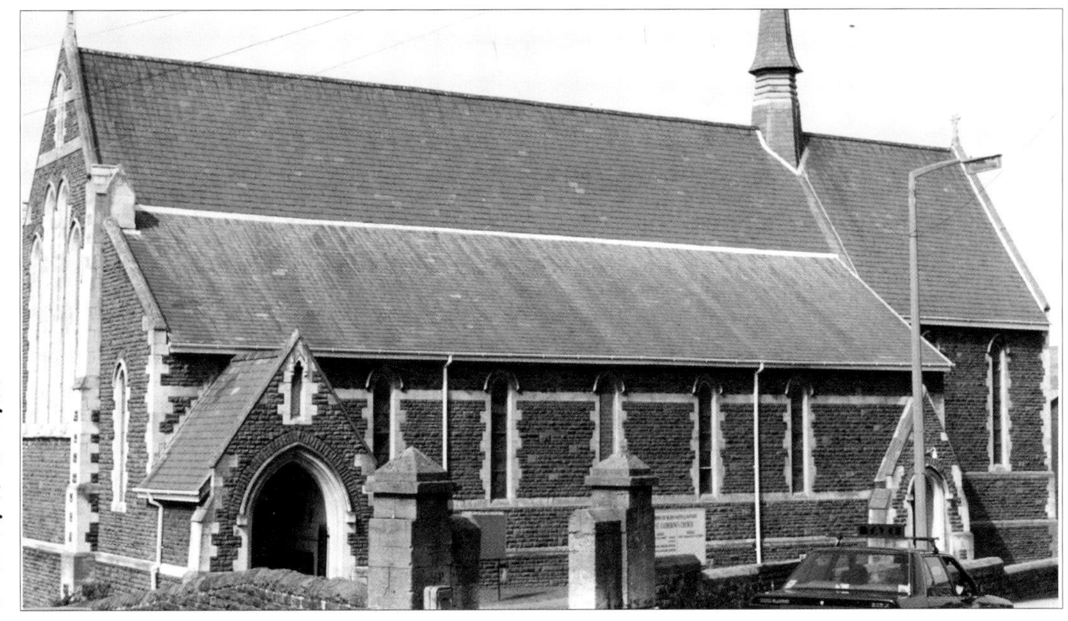

The imposing presence of St Catherine's Church at the junction of Old Road and School Road.

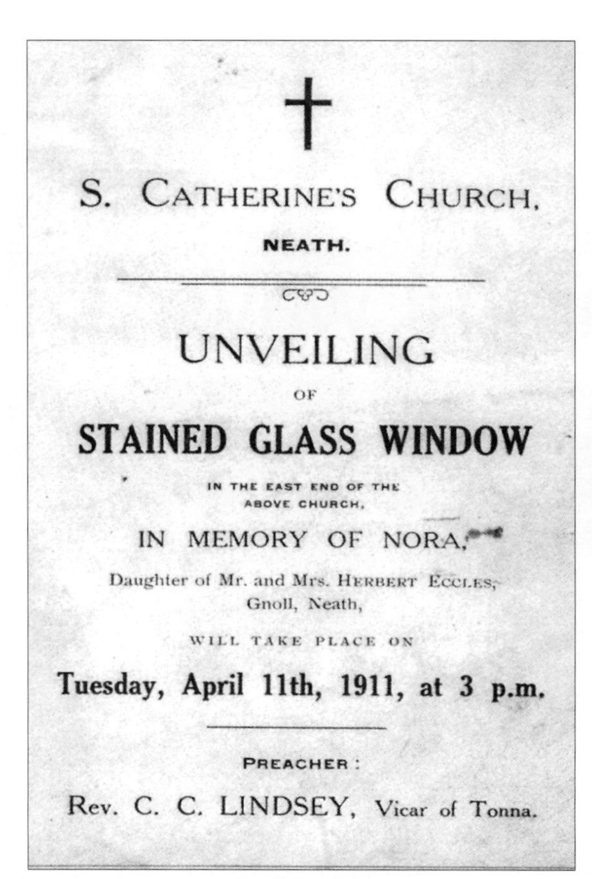
S. CATHERINE'S CHURCH,

NEATH.

UNVEILING

OF

STAINED GLASS WINDOW

IN THE EAST END OF THE
ABOVE CHURCH,

IN MEMORY OF NORA,

Daughter of Mr. and Mrs. HERBERT ECCLES,
Gnoll, Neath,

WILL TAKE PLACE ON

Tuesday, April 11th, 1911, at 3 p.m.

PREACHER:

Rev. C. C. LINDSEY, Vicar of Tonna.

The cover of a commemorative booklet for the unveiling ceremony of a new stained glass window at St Catherine's Church on April 11, 1911.
The window was in memory of Nora, daughter of Mr and Mrs Herbert Eccles of Gnoll House.

To coincide with the May Day in Melincrythan celebrations, a flower festival was held in St Catherine's Church in May 1986. It was organised by church members of the Parish of Neath with Llantwit and their friends. Among many arrangements, the one seen here was dedicated to Youth Clubs and the Boys Brigade.

St Catherine's Church Boys Brigade at Kenfig Hill during a church parade around 1946. The bandsmen are Michael Moody, Donald Pickering, Geoffrey South, David Walters, Keith Davies, Simon Allan, Alan Tandy, Keith Jones, Leslie Oliver, Bernard Hart, Brian Harris, Clayton Phillips, Terry Hunkin, Malcolm Edwards, Donald Bowen, Graham Jones and Raymond Davies.

Brian Harris, Ken Chapple and Clayton Phillips represented St Catherine's Church Boys Brigade in a summer camp, at Weston-Super-Mare for the South Wales Dioceses in 1948.

Members of St Catherine's Church Boys Brigade proudly displaying their cup and certificate, which reads 'South and Central Wales and Monmouth Ambulance Challenge Cup 1930. Winners First Neath Company Boys Brigade.' The man with the moustache is William Gallanders, the father of Ron Gallanders, who was the captain of the brigade. Two of the others are Harold Hale and Stan Davies.

The Boys Brigade started at St Catherine's in 1920 and there were more than 100 members at one time. There were also a section for the younger members called the Life Boys. Lots took place at the Parish Hall, now Melincrythan Community Centre, where they met. One successful activity was gymnastics. The Boys Brigade also went camping every year to Weston Super Mare.

The St Catherine's Church Boys Brigade will be remembered for its outstanding band. Every Sunday they would march from the Parish Hall down Exchange Road, along the main road and up School Road, to the Church for the service, playing all the way.

Mr. Ron Gallanders

Ron Gallanders, a wonderful gentleman, involved in so many facets of church and community life was born in the Melin. He served in the RAF during the Second World War and afterwards worked for a while in Woolworths, before joining the N&C Luxury Coach company, where he became traffic manager until retirement. He was a Neath Borough Council councillor for four years, and a founder member of the May Day in Melincrythan festival.

For almost 40 years, Ron held the office of church warden, for the 'with Llantwit' part of the parish, before becoming sub warden for St Catherine's when the Parish was re-organised. Ron was a pillar of the church and for the members of St Catherine's, he was more than this. Together with his wife, Edith, he was the glue that held the church together. The Church Missionary Society, Christian Aid and Neath Council of Churches, all benefited enormously from his long and detailed involvement, as did the Melin community at large.

When children flocked to a wedding with a difference

These children had come from every corner of the Melin in 1935 to take part in a Band of Hope concert held in Siloh Church hall, Danygraig Road.

More than 80 of them took part in an event called The Doll's Wedding. The Minister, Professor DJ Davies is pictured, along with conductor, Johnny Williams and pianist, Blod Roach.

The bride was Glenys Anthony. David Jenkins, later the secretary at Siloh, was one of the sailors. His wife, Audrey, then aged five, took the part of a mother.

The bridesmaids were Winnie Stinchcombe, June Harris, Stella Dennis, Mair Harris and Joan Elias. The part of a soldier was taken by Danny Davies.

Others performing were Megan Lewis, Margaret Hendra, Beryl Veale, Pam Harris, Lucritia Hopkins, Mary Snow, Janie Bessell, Glan Hughes, Ronnie Bessell, Ken Davies, Dilys Morgan, Jean Pawley, Beryl Pawley, John Jones, Audrey Bond, Molly Evans, Gwyn Rees, Mildred George, Nita Jarret, Mair Rees, Mair Jones, Margaret Jones, Betty Evans, Joan Davies, Doreen Davies, Barbara Pawley, Joyce Evans, Pam Hopkins, Jean Elias, Betty Hughes, Glennie Elias, Meirwen Williams, Ronnie Phillips, David Jenkins, Norman Wybron, Cyril Phelps, Elfed Rees, Anita Jones, Glen Snow, Ron Evans and Idris Evans.

Members of the Siloh Church Drama Group, who performed the play White Collar in the 1940s. Pictured are, back row, from left: Harry Hughes, Sam Arnold, Bessie Rees, WJ Rees, Mrs Edith Lewis, Arthur Davies, David Huckridge, Will Huckridge, Rev Gwyn Lewis, Jim Hughes, Hilda Rees, and Tom Jenkins. Front row: Gwyn Rees, Olive Griffiths, Mair George, Gordon Williams, Brynley Griffiths, Margaret Shute, Joan Lewis and Hugh Griffiths. The young boy is Lloyd Rees.

The children's choir of Siloh Sunday School in the 1930s. Pictured are, back row, from left: Martha Griffiths, Towyn Jones, Dilys Bevan, Vernon Jones, Beryl Davies, Reggie Davies, May Parr and Idris Jarrett. Middle Row: Ken Huckridge, Alan Smith, Mervyn Thompson, David Huckridge, Selwyn Dobbs and Willie Rees. Front row: Anita Jarrett, Betty Parker, Nan Parker, Valerie Jones, Mary Evans and Mary Bessell.

Members of Siloh Chapel, about to start a march to celebrate its centenary in 1980. They marched from Siloh Fach in Danygraig Road, to the big Siloh Chapel on Old Road. Among them are Elfed Rees, editor at the time of the Neath Guardian, Gertrude John, Melin School teacher; Selwyn Dobbs, Keith Mort, Bryn Griffiths, Phil Evans and Danny Evans.

Women of Siloh Chapel during its centenary in 1980. The two men at the back are the Rev EP Howells and Michael Williams, organist. Among the women are Hilda James, Nita Hayward, Hilda Rees, Beryl Holwill, Joan Williams, Blod Roach, Dilys Dobbs, Martha Langford, Mary Hughes, Eluned Richards, Thelma Bridgeman, Doris Phelphs, Gertrude John, Anwen Jones, Pat Williams and Beryl Miles.

Pastor SD Huntley with elders, deacons and trustees of Elim Church in Crythan Road in 1985 on the occasion of its Golden Jubilee. They are, from the left: John Yates, deacon, Clive Ball, deacon; Llew Morris, elder; Pastor Huntley, Bryn Williams, trustee; Jim Clark, deacon; Ernest Challacombe, elder and Wayne Carpenter, Sunday school superintendent.

Young Crusaders at Elim Pentecostal Church, taken around 1953-54. One of the men is Pastor Walker. Among the others are Pat White, Lew Morris, Bryn Williams, Zena Mortimore, Tom Mortimore, Edna Thomas, Megan Phillips, Netta Sparkes, Mrs Jenkins, Glenys Morris, Margaret Morris, Nina Green, Vera Clark, Jim Clark, Ron Phillips, Muriel Phillips, David Griffiths, Ronwen Jones, Jenny Mayers, Mrs Mort, Vi Carpenter, Glenys Newbury, David Newbury and Joe Newbury.

This picture was taken outside the Salvation Army Building in Marshfield Road, in 1948. The building was demolished in the early 1970s to make way for Bowen Street redevelopment. All the women are members of the Corps Sisterhood seen with their new commanding officers. Sitting extreme right in the front is Mrs Newbury, who had the Bakery in Marshfield Road next to Paddy's Club. Lynette Chubb is one of the babies, with her mother Dolly. The other baby is John Turner with his mother Millie. Among others are Gladys Evans and Mrs. Leycock from Penrhiwtyn; Mrs Webley from Marshfield Road; Mrs Violet Lane from Union Street, Penydre; Lizzie Arrowsmith and Gladys Phillips from Neath; Mrs Lloyd from Payne Street; Mrs Thomas Metcalfe from Llantwit; Betty Plant from Old Road; Mrs Pearce, always remembered for delivering newspapers in the Melin and Mrs Carpenter grandmother of of Rev Wayne Carpenter of Bethel Elim.

Members of New Maria Congregational Church with Rev. Idris Vaughan at the opening and dedication of the extension at the church in 1989. Rev Vaughan opened and dedicated the building and Pastor Alan Michael , on the extreme right, conducted the service. The old church building was demolished in 1969 to make way for Neath's new Southern Link road. It was during this period that the church went through a very difficult time. They worshipped at the Old Age Pensioners Hall in Wellfield while their new building was constructed, but this burned down and all their bibles and hymn books were lost. The Salvation Army came to their assistance and leased the church members their hall in Marshfield Road. Eventually they returned to their new church in 1973.

Marching down Windsor Road on Whit Monday around 1946, are children of Ebenezer Chapel, Herbert Road. Among them are Gerald Williams, Noreen Loader, Barry Cox, Dilwyn Thomas, Gerald Harris, Norma Jones, George Sly, Norma Davies, Carol Parry, Joyce Gray, Mair Rees, Glen Ball, Pat Evans, Vivian Lake, Val Griffiths, Sheila Davies, Peter Tomlinson, Marian Carter and Mrs. Bishop. The young girl being carried by her mother is Elizabeth Evans.

Ethel and Cecil Street Mission Sunday School taking part in the Whitsun procession around 1946. George Penny from Cecil Street ran the Sunday School. Uncle George as he was known can be seen marching with the children. They are Jean Allen, Georgie Allen, Sidney Williams from Cecil Street who emigrated in 1947 at the age of 11 with his mother Alma Pascoe, to Canada. Sadly he died in his early 40s due to an accident in work. Others pictured are Margaret Knight, Betty Williams, Norma Jones, Ray Jones, Hazel Jones, June Pascoe, Pamela Watkins, Anita Williams, Joan Williams, Marlene Williams, Bertram Williams, Larry Davies, David Thomas, Terry Francis, Shirley Francis, Carol Pontin, John Jarvis, Denzil Taylor and finally Ann Thomas from Marshfield Road. This young lady later married the TV personality Michael Aspel.

Outside New Maria Congregational Church during Neath Sunday School Union's Teaching Day are, from left: Brian Hughes, Bob Daniel, Brian Worthington, Gwyneth Melville, Rev Alan Michael, President of the Sunday Schools Union; Julia Walker, Sheila Stevens and Arthur Imbrey, editor of Go Teach.

Young Crusader Paul Austin with the Crusaders of New Maria Congregational Church in 1991, presenting a cheque for £342 which was raised by a sponsored walk to Mr Geoff Sparkes, Chairman of South West Wales Visually Impaired Children Take Action.

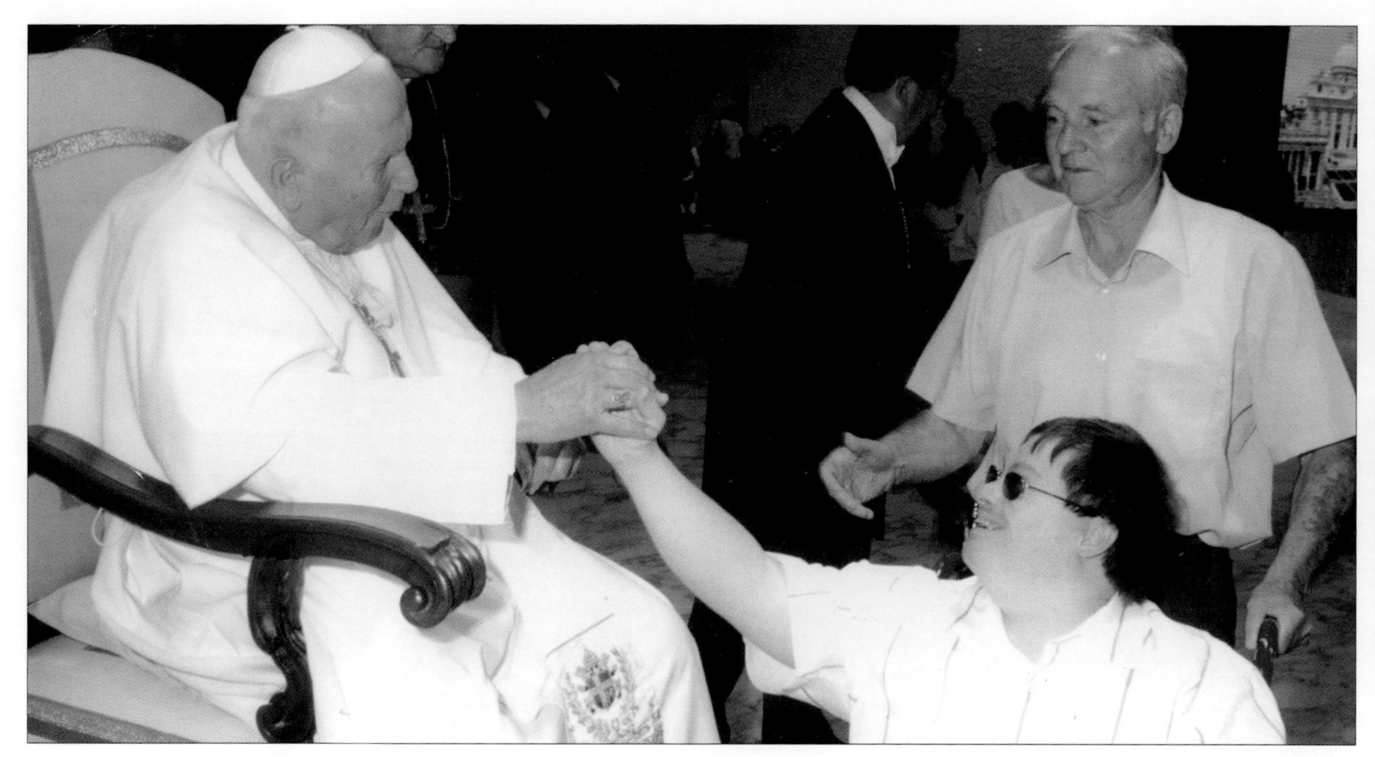

What a moment this was for Richard Evans of Jenkins Road when, on June 23, 2004, he had an audience with Pope John Paul II in the Vatican. With Richard is William, his friend from Port Talbot. Richard was accompanied by his mother Peggy and they were fortunate to be invited to join this trip to Rome by the Nuns of the Stella Maris Convent, Swansea. Richard has Down's Syndrome and for years attended the Abbey Training Centre. Richard was never able to speak properly. He could only be understood by those close to him. For 18 years he travelled to Lourdes and it was in 1996 that his prayers were answered and with the help of doctors in Neath Hospital, he was able to speak more clearly. His mother Peggy said the first clear words he spoke were "I'd like to see the Pope." So this was a dream come true for Richard and his mother. His audience lasted quite a few minutes. Richard even asked the Pope if he was feeling better as he had been unwell. Everyone at St Joseph's Church, where Richard has attended since a child, were thrilled at this meeting.

Representing various churches in Neath these women were cooking and selling Welsh cakes in the Wales Gas showroom in Queen Street for Christian Aid in the early 1960s. Among them are May Llewellyn, Neath Christian Aid secretary, Mary Hughes, Blod Roach, Katy Davies, Hilda Lodge and Lil Lodge.

Work being carried out on Neath Methodist Church at Stockham's Corner in 2005. The church was built in 1913 and opened in 1914. It was built by subscription of one penny for one brick, hence the fact that it is often referred to as the 'Penny Brick' church.

St Joseph's Roman Catholic Church Choir in 1906. Some of the choir members were Robert Croke, Annie O'Sullivan, Kate O'Sullivan, Lizzie O'Sullivan, Maggie O'Sullivan, James O'Sullivan, Mortimer O'Sullivan, Nellie Garbally, Sarah Garbally, Marian Garbally, James Murphy, Father Blackbrough, Lewis Croke, Mary O'Sullivan, Mary Ann Croke, Jim Garbally, and his wife Marian. Jim kept a shoe repair business in Briton Ferry Road, next to the Cambrian pub. When the Catholic Club, known to all as Paddy's Club opened, Jim and Marian were its first Steward and Stewardess. Another person in the photograph was Will Scholard, he was from Old Henry Street and was employed at the Melin Works.

Bethel C.M. Church, Melyn-crythan, Neath, on Sunday, May 20th, 1934 : : : :

MEMORIAL

Singing Festival

to commemmorate the death of

Mr. TOM DUMMER,

M.P.S., F.N.A.O

Conductor, Mr. MATTHEW W. DAVIES, B.A., Mus.Bac., Neath.

Accompanists :

Miss Irene James, A.L.C.M. and Mr. G. Gwynne Waldin.

Chairman: Afternoon, at 2.30 p.m., Ald. J. B. WILLIAMS.

Chairman : Evening at 6 p.m : T. WALDIN. H.M.I.M.

Eulogy written by Mr Reginald Davies, B.A.

Rendered by Miss Vera Shipton.

Stacey Bros., Printers, Neath.

Admission by Programme - 3d.

Tom Dummer

Tom Dummer was associated with the highest forms of musical culture, for a period of over 30 years, as a vocalist and conductor of choirs. He was born one of 10 children in Eva Street. When he married he and his wife lived in Beechwood Avenue. Tom was a chemist and his shop was in Briton Ferry Road, which later became Charles the Chemist. For 23 years he was a conductor of singing at Bethel Church and a Sunday school teacher for over 30 years. He died in 1934, in his 40s. On Whit Sunday, May 20, 1934, a memorial singing festival was held at Bethel Church, Melincrythan, to commemorate his life. Many eminent artists took part. They were assisted by Neath Harmonic Society with conductress Madame Winnie Richards Thomas. Mr. Dummer was the chairman of the Music Committee of the National Eisteddfod of Wales which was held in August 1934, only three months after this Memorial Festival.

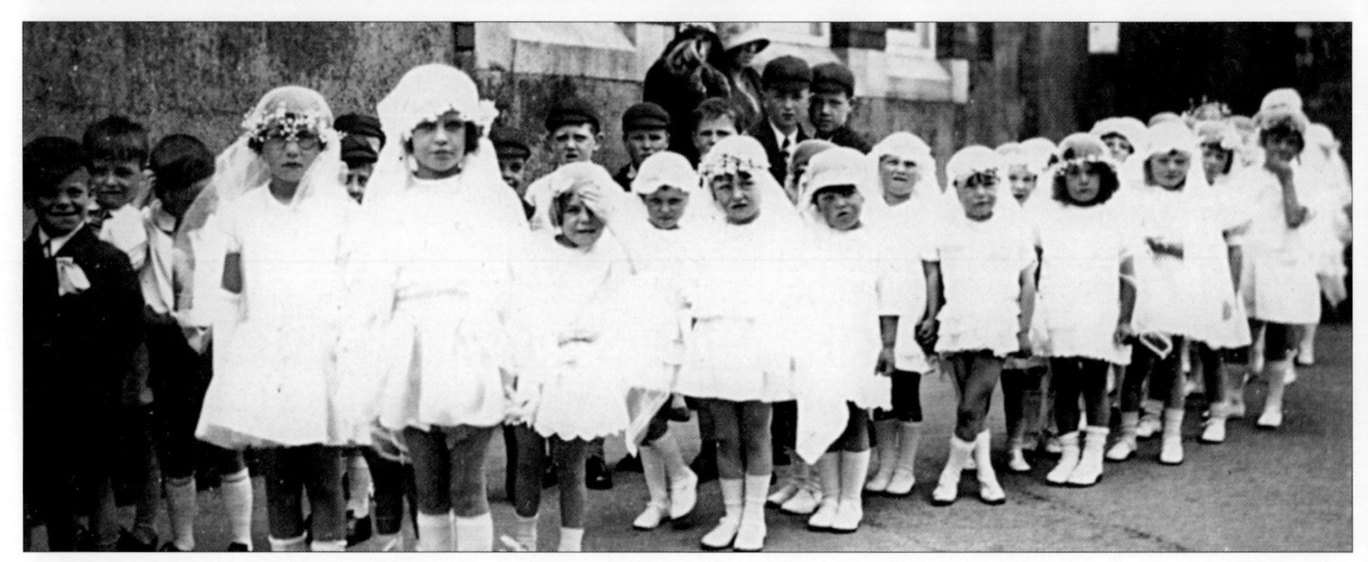

A Corpus Christi procession outside St Joseph's Catholic School, Pendrill Street, 1929. In the front on the right is Joanna Williams and the third girl is Eileen Pascoe.

Chapter 9

Sporting spirit

If anyone needed proof of the sporting prowess of the Melin they need look no further than the list of footballing stars who have begun their careers playing for local teams. Other sports too seem to have looked to the area for future talent.

The origins of this competitive spirit go way back as this photograph of the Melin Stars Football Team in 1917 shows. They are pictured outside the gasworks wall, in the Millands. Among them are David Williams treasurer; W Jenkins, W Parry, Sid Parr, J Prothero, SC Croydon, Tom Beynon, W Knight, trainer; JH Croydon, T Melin, H Anthony, vice captain; Jack Thomas, captain; A Anthony and Ben Parry. Harry Croydon from Skewen was brought up in Mary Street. He contacted me after seeing the picture in my column saying his father Sidney Croydon and his grandfather John Croydon were both in it. His father is one of the players proudly wearing his jersey with the star logo on.

His grandfather John who worked in the Galv can be seen seen wearing a suit and tie and had probably been watching his son play. Harry's father Sidney was born in 1900 so this makes him 17 years old when the photo was taken. Not long after this he had joined and was in the thick of the First World War. Another caller was Betty

Parry, she and her sister Nesta are the two daughters of Benjamin Parry from Pendrill Street, one of those Melin Stars footballers.
Her father's brothers were also in the team. Edward had no children and William had four, Arthur, Gwyn, Raymond and Joan. Finally Mrs Peggy Evans rang from Jenkins Road. Peggy informed me that her father Jack Thomas was the captain of the Melin Stars Football Team in 1917 and can be seen in the photo with the ball. The family was from Pendrill Street. Peggy's mother was seriously injured when their home was bombed during the Blitz in the Second World War.

Melyncrythan RFC, had a successful time and ended up as cup winners in the 1922-23 season. Back row, from left: committee R Williams, J Ball, W Newman, BP Morgan and A Hopkins. Middle row: R Matthews, trainer; WH Hinder, treasurer; HL Bruce, T Llewellyn, A Williams, H Dargavel, S Freeman, W Johns and M Lawrence. Front row: H Bray, L Watkins, Dai Bray, W Rees, T Richards, captain; V Francis, G Clarke, JE Cole, H D Denby, vice captain; On floor: G Elias and P Davies.

This was the Eaglesbush works rugby team during the 1939 season when their kit was gold and blue squares with a white eagle emblem. This team was undefeated at their home ground at Cefn Saeson. Names that are known are Morton Smith, George Vickery, Tom Hughes, captain; Ben Jones, Mayo Abraham, Tom Webber, Charlie Harris, Jimmy Selby, Willie Davies, Charlie Bryce, David Webber, George Vickery, Glyn Ward, Steve Jones and Billy Gibb Davies who can be seen standing extreme right. Billy, from Penydre lost his life in the Second World War when he went down with the Battleship HMS Hood when it was sunk by the German battleship Bismark.

The Eaglesbush rugby team 1948-49. It was taken at Cefn Saeson playing fields which at the time were owned by the Eaglesbush Tinplate Works. The man in the suit kneeling on the right is secretary Dennis Rees. Among the players are Dave Gormon, who loaned the photo, Ivor Jones, Vernon Challinor, Vernon Emanuel, John Pavey, Trevor Giddings, Rowland Richards and Theo Brooks.

Garthmor AFC, the Neath League Premier Division Champions 1935-36. Pictured standing are: B Harris, A Rees, E Gammon, N Whitenman, J Rees, E Pascoe, E Bowen, I Bessell, A McGulloch, P Thomas, H Thomas, H Breech, T Hale, H Clarke and J Rees. The Garthmor team was still in existence in 1950, winning the championship once again in the 1949-50 season.

The Melin Stars AFC team who were finalists in the Neath League Cup and the Burton Cup in the 1946-47 season. Photographed outside the Eaglesbush Inn they are: back row, from left: W Simpson, referee; committee members DL Davies, W Youatt, W Harris, Tom Egan, chairman; D Thomas, W Savage, S Watkins, and G Clarke, secretary. Middle: F Mellin, trainer, D Clarke, Les Egan, Dennis Newton, Dennis Gammon senior, Cyril Harrison, JJ McDonnell, player coach; W Griffiths, treasurer and Bill Griffiths, Eaglesbush landlord. Front: Bertie Williams, C Randall, Lou Youatt, captain; Danny Clifford, Elwyn Colwill. The two young boys are David Youatt and David Clarke.

The Melin Stars football team in the 1947-48 season. Back row, from left: Georgie Clark, Bertie Melin, William Nicholas, Ken Jenkins, Elwyn Colwill, Frankie Francis, Dennis Newton, Tom Egan, Cyril Pascoe, David Colwill. Middle: Lou Youart, F Clifford, Freddie Bracey. Front: Garfield Williams, Albert Williams, Bert Williams, Ken James and Jimmy Briffen.

Penrhiwtyn AFC who were Neath League champions at the end of a successful 1947-48 season. Standing, from left: Ron Jones, committee; John Thomas, Cyril Morris, Harold Chambers, Arthur Robathan, Roy Thomas, Stan Jones and Will Chamber, secretary. Seated: David Davies, Ron Hutchings, Vernon Hendra, Doug Jones and Billy Joseph.

Neath Athletic FC players in 1948. They are: George Gammon, Glen Snow, Ken Smart, Jimmy Smith, Johnny Spagna, John Thomas, Johnny Hutchinson, Billy Haggert, Roy Dunford and Phil Davies.

The Neath Athletic FC team which played in Division Two of the Welsh League in the 1952-53 season. Standing, from left: F Mellin, trainer; E Jones, J Dummer, S Mayers, D Pickerell, V Cook and B Gorman, committee. Seated: G Clarke, secretary; G Holwill, committee; J Spagna, R Jones, captain; R Owen, G Bowen, B Holwill, treasurer. Front: I Penny and C Bell.

Melyn Dynamos, 1948. Back row: Joe Farmer, Francis Clifford, Dennis Edwards, Raymond Jenkins, Dennis Newton, Gwyn Jones, Con Emmit, Bill Williams. Front: Vernon Phillips, Bertie Williams, David Newton, Les Egan, Ron Jones and S Harrison.

A mid-1950s Melin Dynamos football team. Among those pictured are Peter Davies, David Harding, John Jarvis, Ray Fellow, Ronnie Jones, Larry Davies, Melville Davies, David Newton and Ronald Jarrett.

Metal Box AFC, 1952. Back, from left: Bert Geoghan, Ken Amphlette, Alan Williams, Roy Jones, Leo Scanlon, Bryn Tucker, secretary. Front: Ivor Bell, Len Amplett, Cyril Pascoe, David Newton and Vernon Hooper.

This picture of the Metal Box factory tug of war team was taken in the in the late 1940s or early 1950s. Among them are Bill Shewry, Ray Clarke, Tom Cattle, Harold Thomas, Lyndon Lewis and Charles Griffiths.

Metal Box tug of war team in action during the company's annual inter-factory sports day in Acton, London.

Siloh Young People's football team, 1970. Among them are Lynn Snow, Stephen Gosney, Wayne Bills, Rowland Harris and Alan Rees, Colin Davies, Gareth Williams, Colin Powell, Stuart Norman and Paul Chambers.

Siloh B football team in the early 1970s. The players are Dewi Thomas, Paul Jones, David Thomas, John Piper, Dai Lilley, Tudor Norman, Peter Davies, Wayne Harris, Kevin Harris, Martin Thomas, Peter Walters, Roberts and Robert Jenkins. The young boy is Kevin Williams.

Formally Herbert Road AFC, this was the renamed Park Rangers in the 1962-63 season.

Back row, from left: Brian Waring, Gerald Williams, Raymond Harris, Noel Whitefoot, Terry Gregory, Unknown, Richard Blackmore, S Stevens, Peter Rees, Russell Long, Bobby Dixon. Front row; Gerald Mead, David Richards, Clive Brooks, David Wathan and David Pascoe.

This was the Royal Exchange football team in the 1980-81 season. Back row, from left: Gerald Williams, Wynn Tamplin, Carl Storey, Peter Gregory, Richard Jackson, Lynn Snow, Jeff James and Malcolm Eckett. Front: L-R; Kevin Williams, Kevin Williams, Tony Williams, Garry Eckett, Chris Holwill and Mark Reynolds. The Royal Exchange Football Club was founded in 1966 by Glen Snow and originally called Siloh FC. It was formed to provide recreation facilities to youth members at Siloh Sunday School and operated as such until 1979 when it changed its name to Royal Exchange FC.

Proudly posing with the winner's trophy is the Gnoll School football team of 1971. They beat Neath Grammar School 4-1 in the cup final. They are, back row, from left: Carl Lazarus, Peter Thomas, Michael Marmount, Andrew Short, Martin Marmount, Andrew Chesterfield, Wayne Thomas. Front: Wayne Jones, David Jones, David Spittle, John Jeffreys and Paul Moses.

This is a photograph of the Co-op County Cricket Team taken in 1931. Pictured are: E Edwards, J Edwards, EM Jones, I Tallamy, E Hughes, G Watkins, EW Martin, V Bishop, I Harry, C Edwards, S Williams and F Headon.

The Red Dragon Relays cricket team in the late 1960s. Standing, from left; Ray Thomas, Dai Richards, Terry Hammett, secretary; Dai Herbert, Colin Marney, Jim Lang, Philip Davies, Wally Sharp, chairman and scorer; Eddie Weller and Ivor Mellin, umpire. Seated: Frank Jones, Billy Rees, Cyril Davies, Terry Whitelock and David Coleman. The Red Dragon Relay Company had its workshop and offices in Eaglesbush and shops in Queen Street and Windsor Road. All disappeared many years ago. The team played in the Neath and District League.

Mount Pleasant Albion AFC, 1947. Among those pictured are: Phil Davies, Ken Hopkins, Ronnie Evans, Cyril Newman, Roy Jones, Billy Walters, committee; Ken Pughsley, committee;Haydn Jenkins, Aubrey Davies, Jimmy Smith and Arthur Wiltshire.

The Mount Pleasant Albion Football Club with players, committee and supporters, 1953. Back row, from left: Freddie Tucker, Gwyn Jones, Gerald Jenkins and Nippy Smith. Middle: Bertie Williams, Darrel Lennon, Ben Thomas, Glyn Williams, Topsy, Walter Banister, Lincoln Phillips, father of Leighton Phillips who captained Aston Villa and Wales. Front: Norman Webb, David Hanford, Eric Becker, Terry McNeil, Tommy Carsley, Jim Brennan, Eddie Pool and Trevor Walters.

Mount Pleasant Albion football team, 1960. Back row: Len Evans, Terry Hooper, Emrys Newton, Terry McNeil, Unknown and Martin Howells. Front: Roy Phillips, Michael Hutchings, David Wassell, Raymond Thomas and Billy Hughes.

Members of the Metal Box cricket team, 1954-55 at Cefn Saeson cricket ground. Back row, from left: David Tucker, umpire; George Gammon, Cyril Foster, Jeff Evans, David Rees and Roy Jones. Seated: Harold Norman, Raymond Thomas, Danny Llewellyn, captain; Sam Jones, Emo Davies and Malcolm Evans.

This photograph was taken outside the Metal Box Sports Club, when the Metal Box cricket team were league champions in 1962. Back row, from left: Len Jordon, Ray Carr, Malcolm Evans, Roy Jones, Norman Whitelock, D Jones, Roy Harris, David Rowlands and L Owen. Seated: Noel Mort, Sam Jones, secretary; P Evans, Malcolm Rogers, captain; Mr Hamilton, Metal Box manager; Alan Richards and John Thomas.

The Remploy cricket team, 1986. Back row, from left: Mark Lewis, Roger Kenerley, T Lewis, Steve Amphlett, David Prior, David Flynn and Dave Saunders. Front: Mark Walsh, Dave Weston, C Tidridge, John Seage and J White. Roger Kenerley represented Wales at bowls in South Africa in 2000 and New Zealand in 2004.

The cricket team of Ebenezer, Herbert Road who were the first winners of the Neath Cricket League in the 1950s. Back row, from left: Brian Waring, Alan Watkins, Gilbert Barnsley, Lloyd Rees, Mervyn Trolley and Cyril Morgan. Middle; Brian Green, David Green, Will Morgan, captain; Alan Jones and Royston Davies. The two on the floor are John Dyer and Gerald Williams.

Members of the Royal Exchange A & B Skittles teams in the mid-1980s. Among them are landlord and landlady, John and Freda Holding, Liz Holding, Martin Rees, Graham Green, Jim Bowditch, Mervyn Blackmore, David Flynn, Terry Profit, Graham Price, Alan Powis, Peter Thomas, Len Palfrey, Alan Brock, Colin Marney, Liam Barry, Ray Jenkins, Terry Williams, Iris Powis, Alun Mellin, Dennis Davies and Steve Griffin.

Melin Social Club skittles team winners, 1980. Standing, from left: Alan Brooks, Dai Watkins, Gary Parsons, Ted Rees, Gilbert Thomas, Harry Collier. Front; Wynford Gillard, Brian Lee, Damien Lloyd, Brynmor Mayers and Terry John.

Neath Royal British Legion Darts Team being presented with the cup for winning the Friends of the Hospital Darts League Tournament in the early 1920s. Presenting the cup to the team captain, Trevor Mogford, is Alderman Aneurin Rees, former Mayor of Neath, who was the first Chairman of Neath Friends of the Hospital. Also present was his wife Mrs Rees, chairman of Briton Ferry Community Council. Others present include Bill James, Malcolm Wiltshire, David Lawrence, Peter Davies, Raymond Davies, Emrys Newton, Jack Brocksopp, Ron Cook, Raymond Lewis, Malcolm Hughes, Tony Diamond and Jackie Evans. The other woman in the picture is Katie Davies who had a shoe shop in the Melin. She was president of the Neath Friends of the Hospital.

A presentation ceremony for the Friday-nighters Darts Team in 1957. The team played every Friday from the Exeter Public House. Seen here are landlord Tudor Burns, landlady Hettie Burns, Stan Jenkins, Evan Humphreys, Stan Brettle, Daryl Veale, Ivor Morgan, Dai Johns, Peter Jones, Leo Davies, Ernie Burgess, Stan Jordan, Okko Harris, David Gregory, Dai Bowen and Walter Mayers.

Members of the Metal Spinning Tigers womens football team in the early 1960s, pictured outside the main gates of the factory. Kathleen Davies of Gnoll Park Road, who was one of the players, sent in the photograph. She related how the women were coached by the toolsetters at the factory. One event she recalled was the time when the manager of Tottenham Hotspur was in the area and went to see them play at Ynysmaerdy. Apart from Kathleen others included above are Jean Rees, Gloria Mogford, Janice Davies and Susan Clarke.

Pictured in action in 1993 is young Welsh acrobat Kerry Hughes from Pendrill Street. Together with her sister Louise and Louise Edwards from Howells Road they went to Germany to take part in the fifth European Circus Festival. The girls plus three from Llanelli were all members of Acro Wales. Kerry along with Leanne Dickeson from Llanelli appeared on an HTV programme called Tribe showing off their skills.

The Mount Pleasant bowls team with their wives in the mid-1950s. The club was the first in the district and funded by employees of the Great Western Railway in 1913. Standing in the centre of the middle row is Samuel Dummer from Danygraig Road, one of the founder members. He was also a county bowls player.

Briton Ferry Athletic FC captain Ray Thomas presents a framed picture to Maldwyn Rees on his retirement as manager and coach.

A line up of Metal Box cricketers past and present in 1981. Back row, from left are: G Carr, Billy Thomas, David Parker, Brian Butler, Len Jordan, Roy Harris, David Rees, Tyrone Elias, Colin Rees, Alan Richards, Norman Rees, Emlyn Williams, David Williams, Andrew Michael, Phillip Michael, Colin Berni, Alun Jenkins, Peter Davies and Jack Anthony. Front: David Rowlands, John Thomas, Ralph Baker, Lyn Owen, Malcolm Rogers, Peter Lester, Peter Rooke, Ray Carr, John Sparkes and David Richards. On the ground: Roy Jones, Brian Rees with Lady the dog.

This was the first Great Western Railway and British Rail snooker team around 1946. Back row, from left: Ben Griffiths, Stan Sayers, Gilbert Thomas, Bill Tustin, Harold Cole, Fred Stiles and Gwyn Jones. Seated: Trevor Powell, Ces Nicholls, Dai Jones, Matt Rees and Harold Richards. The men at the back were spectators.

Chapter 10

Ace of clubs

At the heart of the Melin is Neath Boys Club, one of the largest of its kind in Wales, and one of the largest independent Youth Clubs in West Glamorgan. The club has many successes to its credit and can claim a proud history and tradition.

It is affiliated to the Welsh Federation of Boys and Girls Groups, the successor to Boys Clubs of Wales, to the National Association of Boy's Clubs, and to the Welsh Association of Youth Clubs. Recounted here is a peep into its history up until 1992 when a new building was opened. The club has a proud history and tradition. It was founded in 1929, when a few policemen of the old Neath Borough Police Force decided to organise activities for the youngsters of the area. The first meeting place was in the Neath Toc Club on the corner of Church Place, opposite the Town Hall. The club soon moved to its present site, its new home being the old clubhouse so recently demolished.

This building had originally been a large chapel, dating back to 1859 and consisting of 12 rooms on two levels. After it ceased to be used as a chapel, the building had been acquired by the Metal Box company, and used as a store. Metal Box initially rented the building to the Boy's Club for a nominal one shilling a week, before eventually donating it to the Club.

The club went from strength to strength in its new home, building up its membership and developing a wide range of activities.

Over the years, it also built up an enviable record of achievement in the world of sport. In particular, its success on the football field has been unrivalled by any club in Wales. No club has come close to matching the success of Neath Boys' Club's teams over the years, while the number of the club's 'old boys' who have gone on to enjoy successful careers in professional football is truly amazing. The club's contribution to the Welsh International Team has been immense.

The mid and late 1980s proved to be a critical period in the club's history. Its building was deteriorating rapidly, and more and more resources were having to be committed to its increasingly uphill battle to stem the advancing tide of decay.

In December 1990, it was learned that the club had been awarded a grant of £150,000 by the Welsh Office, to demolish the old building and to build a new headquarters on the site. Demolition of the old building commenced on April 3, 1991. In the period between then and the opening of the new building, the club continued to function, holding club nights at the nearby Melincrythan Community Centre.

The new building was officially opened on February 3 1992, by the Mayor of Neath, councillor WR Williams.

In January that year, the name of the club had been officially changed to Neath Boys and Girls Club.

The mural on the front of the building was painted by members of the Club in 2005, with the support of club leaders, artist Rubin Eynon and Neath Port Talbot Youth Service, who financed the project. The conservatory was built in April 2007 and dedicated to the memory of Graham Wathan who gave up so much of his free time for the Boys and Girls of the Melin. The club's womens section, whose fund raising efforts over many years made this and so many other things possible have always been an enormous support.

Goodbye old Boys Club. Danygraig Road can be seen in the distance, after its demolition.

Hello new Boys Club, opened in 1992!

This photograph of members of Neath Boys Club was taken on October 2, 1938, on the extreme right is one of the policemen of the old Neath Borough Police Force who founded the club in 1929, when he and a group of colleagues decided to organise activities for the youngsters of the area.

A visit to Neath Boys Club by the Duke of Gloucester in the 1950s.

Members of Neath Boys Club dressed as miners for a fund raising event in 1937. Back row: Bertie Williams, Frankie Jones, John Jones, Gwyn Harris, Dai Thomas, Clifford Chambers and Idris Penny. Front row: Doug Harris, Douglas Mogford, Vernon Davies, Randall Bridle and Harry Weeks.

The Melin Boys Club football team outside the Boys Club in the mid-1930s. In the picture are Les Jones, Tom Jones, Glyn Williams, Ken Davies, Jimmy Smith, Albert Harris, VG Ellis, Stan Arbour, Idris Jarrett, Jim Evans, Tom Egan, Rod Evans, Garfield Jones, area organiser Welsh Boys Clubs; Idris Penny, Ron Evans captain; Len Jordan, Sammy Lane, Mr Leyshon Williams, caretaker and leader of the club, known to all as 'Dad Williams'; Cyril Evans, Gordon Davies and Len Heard. Len was a spectator and his great friend was the captain of the team, Ron Evans. They were both from Curtis Street. At the start of the Second World War these two mates went to Swansea to join up. They hoped to be in the forces together, but Ron was accepted in the Royal Navy and Len the Royal Marines. They both survived the war to continue their friendship.

All these young boys were photographed on the stairs in the old Neath Boys Club in 1956. From the top down they are: Alun Mellin, Bryn Vaughan, Robert Joseph, Graham Price, Bobby Turner, David James, Wilfred Clarke, Martin Howells, Elfed Pugh, Dilwyn Evans, Martin Wagstaff, Roger Mead, Eddie Soper, Dai Richards, John Bowen, John Jones, Peter Bramley, Brian Harrison, Tyrone Elias, Gomer Lewis, Ron Jones, Dai Quant and Dilwyn Evans.

A wartime Neath Boys Club football team outside the Neath Cricket Club pavilion in the 1942-43 season. Back row, from left: N Edwards, J Hopkin, leader and CJ Harrison. Middle row: H Davies, A Parry, D Newton, K Jenkins, S Penny, L Phillips. Front: B Williams, I Penny, M Rees, captain; E Breech and D Harris.

A Neath Boys Club football team in 1952. Back row, from left: John Case, Malcolm Wiltshire, Raymond Langan, David Wassell, Graham Green, Emrys Newton and Peter Roderick. Front kneeling; D. Byers, Brian Davies, Malcolm Davies and George Morgan.

Neath Boys Club under 12s Champions 1965-66. Back row, from left: Mr D Evans, Mr A Vaughan, Mr D Collins, Mr J Flynn, Dennis Vaughan, Ernie Binding, Nicky Jenkins, Paul Collins, Richard Rees, Paul Emmanuel and Colin Rees. Front row: Peter Hill, Andrew Christie, Chris Pugh, David Semmens, Brian Flynn and Wayne Harris.

Neath Boys Club under 16s football team in 1967. Pictured are from left, back row: Mr Butson, Bill Newlands, Robert Walters, Stephen Mascetti, Martin Jenkins, Peter Rosser, Jeff David and George Singleton. Front: Mike Parfitt, Chris Newlands, Keith Butson, Peter Gray, Paul Semmens and Robert Michael.

Neath Boys Club under 16s team in 1966. They were winners of the Boys Club of Wales Cup, the Neath and Port Talbot League Cup and the Stacey Shield. Standing, from left are: Barry Colwill, Paul Timms, Donald Wileo, Michael Williams, Graham Morgan and Robert Colwill, and seated; Michael Parsons, Keith Hutchings, Kevin James, Brian Rees and Byron Edwards.

Neath Boys Club under 12s Team in 1976 at the Barn training complex at Hengwrt. They are Julian Vaughan, John Chick, Danny Watkins, Roger Rouse, Keith Burt, Alan Sullivan, Gareth Stanton, Peter Michael, Peter Howells, captain; Huw Davis and Martin Hughes.

This Neath Boys Club under 13s team were winners of the Neath League and League Cup. Kneeling from left are: Jonathan Finn, Gary Cole, Paul Carpenter, Richard Michael, captain; Wayne Curtis, Grant Watkins and Stuart Collier. Standing are: Darren Walters, Darren French, Craig Richards, Ian Derrick, Nicholas Davies, Jason Davies, Wayne Gittins, Simon Harris, Richard Jones, Paul Howard and Christopher Harries.

Neath Boys Club's management committee, 1992. Back row, from left: Rita Williams, Malcolm Hazel, Christine Pickrell, Joan Wathan, Moria Thomas, Glyn Thomas, John Holding and Ian Hale. Seated: George Eaton, Graham Wathan, Bill Newlands, Dave Beynon, Diane Hazel, Marian Eaton and Dennis Curtis.

Mayor Gerald Hemmings at a Neath Boys Club presentation evening, 1971. pictured with President Mr Idris Hale and members of the management committee, guests and Mrs Ivy Thomas who was a tireless worker for the club.

President of Neath Boys Club, Idris Hale, presents a cheque to Mrs Ivy Thomas during a visit by Frankie Vaughan to Penscynor, Cilfrew, 1974. Pictured from left are: June Hughes, Jean Sharpe, Val O'Keefe, Ivy Thomas, Alec Vaughan, George Singleton, Gillian Evans, Ivor Evans, Frankie Vaughan, Idris Hale, Chief Supt. Ron Rees and Bill Newlands.

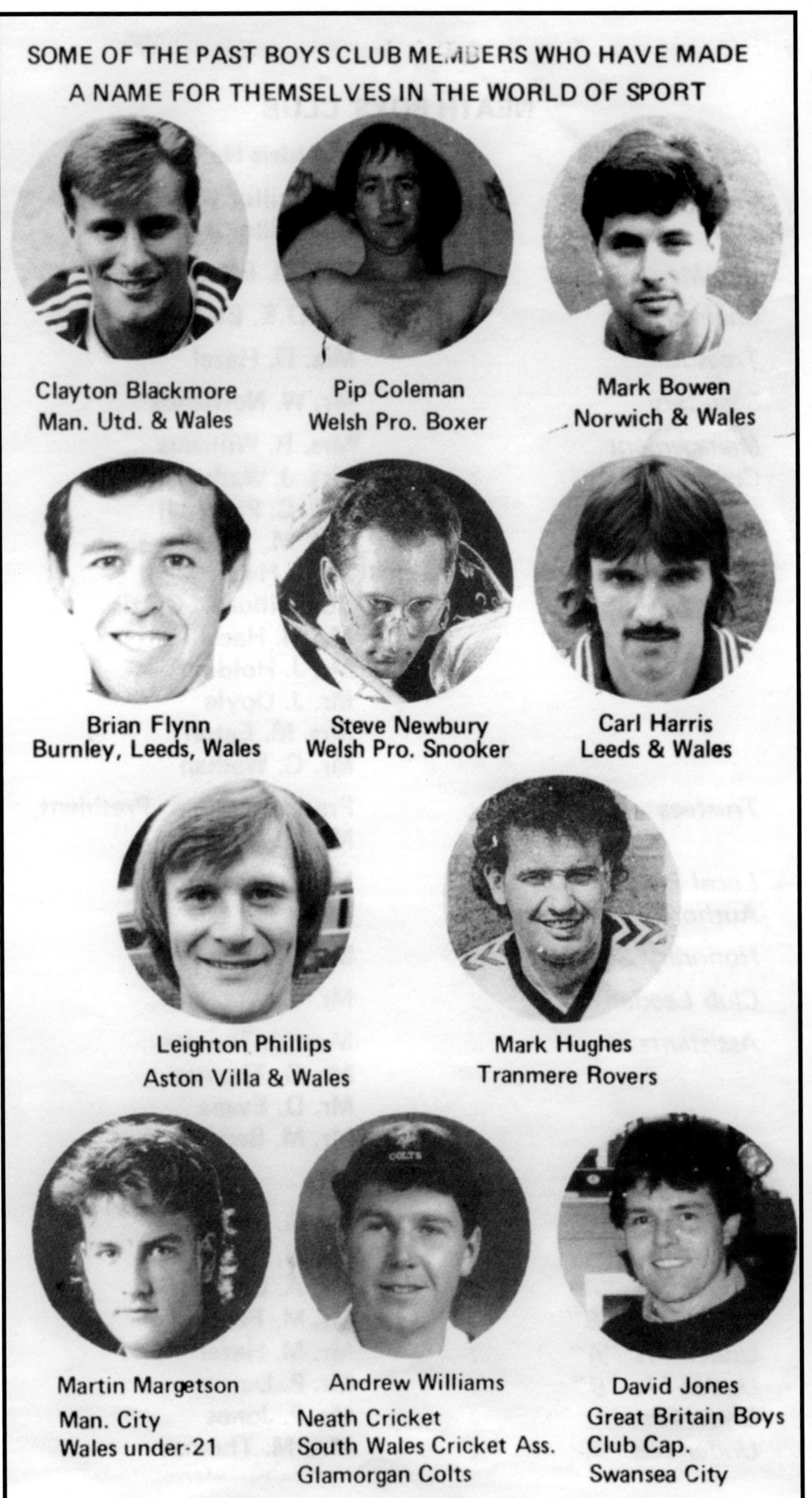
SOME OF THE PAST BOYS CLUB MEMBERS WHO HAVE MADE A NAME FOR THEMSELVES IN THE WORLD OF SPORT

Clayton Blackmore
Man. Utd. & Wales

Pip Coleman
Welsh Pro. Boxer

Mark Bowen
Norwich & Wales

Brian Flynn
Burnley, Leeds, Wales

Steve Newbury
Welsh Pro. Snooker

Carl Harris
Leeds & Wales

Leighton Phillips
Aston Villa & Wales

Mark Hughes
Tranmere Rovers

Martin Margetson
Man. City
Wales under-21

Andrew Williams
Neath Cricket
South Wales Cricket Ass.
Glamorgan Colts

David Jones
Great Britain Boys
Club Cap.
Swansea City

The cover of a commemorative souvenir programme of a special day for the Melin.

SOUVENIR PROGRAMME TO COMMEMORATE THE OPENING OF THE NEW

NEATH BOYS CLUB

Officially opened by:
HIS WORSHIP THE MAYOR OF NEATH
COUNCILLOR W. R. WILLIAMS

MONDAY, FEBRUARY 3rd, 1992

One of the pages from the commemorative programme.

Tony Pickerell, who played for Wales Youth at every level and Cardiff City AFC.

Neath Boys Club under 12s champions, 1990-1991. Back Row, from left: Moira Thomas, manager; Brian Hopkins, assistant manager; Lee Ward, Richard Knight, Christian Morris, Craig McNeil, Simon Black, Ross Livingstone, Ian Vaughan and Nigel Scott. Front: Chris Taylor, Andrew Thomas, Andrew Price, Gareth Bevan, Lee Hopkins and Mark Davies.

Proudly sporting their new soccer kit, sponsored by Neath and District Darts League, are a Neath Boys and Girls Club Football Team. Pictured are, back row, from left: Emma Lewis, Rachel Perrott, Sarah Collins, Karen Cummins, manager: Rachel Rogers, Kimberley Michael, captain; Clare Powell and Sharon Mathews. Front: Nicole Brown, Emma Davies, Claire Topper, Victoria Cummings, mascot; Angela Mead, Sharon Youatt and Tracey Baker.

Pictured in the late 1970s are these excited youngsters who had a morning off school to meet a pair of famous footballers and be presented with autographed soccer balls. The players involved were Francis Lee, former Manchester City and England player and Dennis Law, former Manchester United and Scotland player. The woman in the picture was Mrs Evans of Rugby Avenue, who was representing her son Geoffrey, who was one of the two winners of a competition run by the Co-op in Neath, where the presentation took place. The other winner was 11 year old Stuart Thomas from Castle Drive, Cimla. The other boys in the picture were outstanding members of Neath Boys Club, accompanied by the leader of the club, Bill Newlands. They were Richard Williams, of Cwrt Sart School, Mark Waites of Gnoll Junior School, Christian Roach, Paul John and David Lee, of Melin School, Stephen Nicholas and Clive Brereton, also of Melin School, Phil Tucker of Cadoxton School and Richard Phillips of Cwrt Sart School.

Neath Boys Club under 13s Team, Port Talbot and District League Champions, 1970-1971. Back row, from left: Neil Spendiff, Conrad Davies, John Chamberlain, Gary Mogford, captain; Mark Evans, Martyn Jones and Neil Thomas. Front row: Eric Marmount, Paul Edwards, Paul Jones, Clive Chambers and Howard Hamer.

This Neath Boys Club team had just won a cup final against Aberavon Boys Club. The venue was Victoria Road, Port Talbot. The date, Easter Monday, 1962. The final score was 7-1 to the Neath Boys and they were presented with their medals by Mel Charles, the brother of John Charles. The successful team were: Barry Colwill, John Kingdom, Peter Clarke, Donald Wilyeo, Dennis Llewellyn, Michael Powell, Terry O'Keefe, Keith Hutchings, Kevin James, Mike Richardson and John Richards.

Neath Boys Club under 13s 1980. Back row, from left: Jason Hardwick, Andrew Phillips, Andrew O'Callaghan, Richard Williams, Richard Williams and Leighton Vickers. Front: Adrian Morely, Mark Fish, Paul Maddocks, Andrew Reynolds, Paul Linciano and Richard Davies.

Neath Boys Club under 12s football team, winners of a competition at Butlins, in 1984. Some of those pictured are; Malcolm Waters, Darren Walters, Paul Carpenter, Keith Davies, Jason Davies, Wayne Curtis, Richard Michael, Jeff Michael, Ian Derrick, Gomer Richards, Craig Richards, Byron Davies, Anthony Brock, Adrian Preece, Lee Marshall, Mr Marshall and Dennis Curtis.

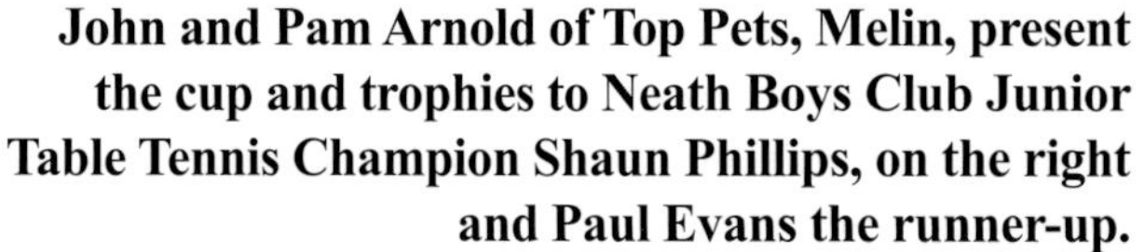

John and Pam Arnold of Top Pets, Melin, present the cup and trophies to Neath Boys Club Junior Table Tennis Champion Shaun Phillips, on the right and Paul Evans the runner-up.

Neath Boys Club bids a sad farewell to its treasurer Marjorie Bradfield, who is pictured on the right receiving gifts from Diane Hazel, left, who takes over the post of treasurer. Next to her is Ladies Committee chairperson Joan Wathan, then Neath Community Council chairman councillor Dennis Curtis, club chairman Dave Beynon, club vice president, councillor George Eaton and secretary, Bill Newlands.

The chairman of Neath Community Council, councillor Dennis Curtis, presents a kit to the chairman of Neath Boys Club, Dave Beynon and football secretary Moira Thomas in 1991. Included in the picture are vice chairman of Neath Community Council, councillor Sheila Penry, councillors Agnes John, Malcolm Gunter, David Huckridge, Glan Pascoe and David Williams; Boys Club leader, Glyn Thomas, secretary; Ian Hale, treasurer; Diane Hazel, Joan Wathan, chairlady of the Ladies Fund Raising committee and Rita Williams, vice chairman.

Money raised by the Neath Workingmen's Club quiz team provided Neath Boys Club football team with a new kit. Seen wearing the outfits are team members Nicholas Hale, Mathew Davies and goalkeeper Ryan O'Rourke. They were at the club to receive the kit and with them are councillor Dennis Curtis, club vice chairman, Martin Phillips; Boys Club secretary, Ian Hale; team manager, Noel Davies and quiz team members John Elliott, Peter Williams, Jim Williams, Diane Hendy, Clive Hendry and Lynn Davies.

A Neath Boys Club presentation evening at the Melin Social Club in the late 1980s. In the picture are David Griffiths, club leader; Clayton Blackmore, Carl Harris and Martin Margetson.

Two Welsh football internationals, Clayton Blackmore, left and Carl Harris, right, with future international Martin Margetson.

NEATH BOYS CLUB BOXING SECTION

PRESENTS

AN EVENING OF ALL-STAR AMATEUR BOXING. W.A.B.A. APPROVED.

AT

THE ROYAL BRITISH LEGION CLUB, BRITON FERRY, NEATH.

MONDAY, OCTOBER 16th. 1989.

TONIGHT'S PROGRAMME WILL FEATURE THE FOLLOWING:

MIDDLEWEIGHT.
SCOTT LAMBOURNE, Neath Boys Club .V. MIKE JONES, Towy

LIGHTWEIGHT
MARK OWEN, Neath Boys Club .V. DENNIS SULLIVAN, Trallwn

LIGHT-HEAVYWEIGHT
ROY BIRD, Neath Boys Club .V. ADRIAN JENKINS, Trallwn

LIGHT-MIDDLEWEIGHT
MIKE TOLTON, Neath Boys Club .V. PETER GALLAGHER, Trallwn

LIGHT-HEAVYWEIGHT
CARL THOMAS, Neath Boys Club .V. DEREK HITCHINS, Rhondda

WELTERWEIGHT
LEE FRANCIS, Neath Boys Club .V. RICHARD LONGMAN, R.A.F.

A boxing tournament programme for an event organised by Neath Boys Club at Briton Ferry in October 1989.